Restless as a Viking

Stephan V. Benediktson

Written by Stephan V. Benediktson
2016

Benson Ranch Inc.
251018 Tower Ridge Estates
Calgary, Alberta
T3Z 2M2

ISBN 13: 978-0-9733657-4-0

Acknowledgements

I am particularly grateful for the assistance in the writing of this book that I received from Jeremy Luke Hill, Vidar Hreinsson and Dr. Kenneth Graham. I am also very grateful for the support that I received from my wife, Adriana, during the time I spent preparing this book and for the host of friends and family and coworkers that have a part in my stories.

I also appreciate all of the fine work done by the Writers' Guild of Alberta to encourage and support writing of all kinds in the Province of Alberta, and beyond. I have been a member of the Alberta Writers Guild since writing my first book in 2003 and since 2006 I have been the Sponsor of the annual Stephan G. Stephansson prize in poetry, awarded by the Writers' Guild of Alberta.

CONTENTS

Preface

The years roll by, and we are a part of events and accumulate experiences and those of us who are fortunate enough to enjoy retirement years inevitably finish doing some things just for the sake of doing them. I have in my retirement years published a few books, travelled, played polo and bridge, collected art and enjoyed the company of a multitude of friends, family and acquaintances; life is good.

Books are very important in the Icelandic culture; I am a born-in-Alberta Canadian of Icelandic descent. As I looked back and thumbed through my files, I decided to compile this book around some of the things that have been important in my life: family, my Icelandic ethnicity, the fascinating oil business, some of my experiences in the oil business and finally sharing some of my opinions on social issues. I thought I would put these experiences in print in large part so my family, now and in the future, could have some record of how it was. I hope that the reader will find something here of interest.

The first section, Some Speeches, is comprised of addresses that I made at various occasions over the years, touching especially on the state of the oil industry in a world with limited supply but ever increasing consumption of oil. The Oil Patch Tales of the second section describe some of my life working in the oil industry and were originally published as a monthly series in *The Roughneck* magazine, starting September 2012. The third part on Family includes letters and other writings that concern my family, particularly my ancestor, The Poet, Stephan G. Stephansson. The final section, Contrarian Views, expresses my opinions on some controversial subjects, and to those who know me, it will come as no surprise that I would love these views to stir some emotional reactions, positive or negative.

I must say how very, very grateful I am for all of my life's experiences. I have had a remarkable run, as they say. Not the least of which was having two life's companions to whom I owe so much: my first wife of over 30 years, a born-in-London Anglo, and my second wife of over 25 years, a born-in-Bogota Latina. Always supportive, the contrasts have added much to my life's experiences.

Stephan Vilberg Benediktson

Introduction

First printed as "Restless as a Viking" by Bruce White in Faculty of Engineering Magazine: *University of Alberta: Winter 2006.*

> Though you have trodden in travel
> All the wide tracts of the earth,
> Bear yet the dreams of your bosom
> Back to the land of your birth.
> – *Stephan G. Stephansson*

As an engineer in his early 40s, Stephan Benediktson (Civil '62) stood at the epicentre of the petroleum age. It was the mid-1970s, when Saudi Arabia poured forth 11 million barrels of sweet, light crude every day – oil to fuel all the Oldsmobile Tornados and Boeing 727s in the world, oil to heat houses so cheaply that it was hardly worth the expense to insulate them properly.

Saudi oil was, and still is, a fantastic source of energy and wealth. A single area, the Abqaiq Production Division, had 220 employees and 300 wells that produced three million barrels a day. To put it into perspective, those 300 wells produced twice as much oil as all of Alberta did at its peak conventional production a decade ago. They pumped out more than all the oil sands mega-projects in Alberta are expected to produce 10 years from now. More than one-quarter of Saudi Arabia's peak oil production came from those 300 wells alone.

At the very heart of this prodigious outpouring of petroleum, University of Alberta graduate Stephan Benediktson was working for Exxon affiliate Aramco as the production superintendent in charge of those 300 wells at Abqaiq. Not bad for a farm boy from the Hecla district west of Innisfail, Alberta, who quit

school at the age of 15. Born in 1933, Stephan Vilberg Benediktson is a grandson of Stephan G. Stephansson, an early Alberta
settler (1889) who was also Iceland's most revered poet. (The
Stephansson house at Markerville is a provincial historic site,
open to visitors in the summer.) When Benediktson was nine
years old his father died, and the son left school in his teens to
find work. Young Stephan ended up working for Imperial Oil
on their rigs from Joffre, Alberta, to Norman Wells, North West
Territories. It was the beginning of the journey that would take
him to Abqaiq and beyond. An exceptionally ambitious young
man, at the age of 24, Benediktson was married and father of the
first of his three children, Steve Jr., when he made the gutsy decision to complete his education. First he returned to high school
in Red Deer, and then he enrolled in Civil Engineering at the
University of Alberta. For five years, he studied and supported
his young family by working on the rigs for Imperial during the
summers and holidays.

As a graduate engineer, he worked for Imperial in Edmonton and Redwater, and then was sent to Exxon's production
research centre in Houston. The family moved in the late 1960s
to Australia, where Benediktson was a part of Exxon's pioneering achievements in offshore oil and gas developments in the
Bass Strait. Next, he was sent to Indonesia in the early 1970s,
soon after the revolution that saw the government of Sukarno
overthrown by the military under Suharto ; Indonesia was memorable for its primitive conditions at the time. He then decided
to take a job in Ottawa helping the government regulate and develop an Arctic oil and gas policy. Then from 1974 to 1977, he
worked for Aramco, an oil company owned by Exxon, Chevron,
Mobil, and Texaco that was in the process of being bought out
by the government of Saudi Arabia.

"I was there when Saudi Arabia peaked in oil production at
11 million barrels per day, and I doubt they will ever reach that
level again," Benediktson says. It is also very unlikely that one
engineer will ever again take charge of 300 wells producing three
million barrels of oil a day. Yet that was all an ordinary day's
work for the ambitious, hard-working Albertan.

Introduction

"We would have a conference call every day at seven in the morning, and there would be two or three vice presidents on the call," he remembers. "You had to report what you produced the day before and what maintenance you needed during the day," as simple as that.

As restless as his ancient Viking ancestors, Benediktson left Saudi Arabia in 1977, but not the oil industry. Over the next three decades he worked in the Calgary oil patch as the vice president of drilling and production in Canada for Amerada Hess Corp. Then, in 1980, he returned to the Middle East as vice president in charge of Hess Corp's operations in the United Arab Emirates. "I've been under water a couple of times in my life and that was one of them," he recalls. "I inherited an offshore production operation, a jack-up drilling rig operation with a major construction project in progress. It was quite a challenge."

In 1983, right after the Falklands War and with a military junta still in power, he moved to Buenos Aires to take charge of the Argentine oil company Bridas – and for the second time found himself out of his depth. At first understanding only two words of Spanish, *si* and *gracias*, he says he didn't know what was going on half the time. There were the challenges of running a business in a hyper-inflated economy. "We gave everybody a cost-of-living raise of between 25 and 35 percent a month. A month! And there was all this wasted time and motion re-negotiating contracts, things like that."

After four years, he returned to Alberta and started Benson Petroleum Ltd., a successful Alberta junior oil company that for a bargain price took over a significant oil field in Colombia. "At the time, people asked, 'What is a little Alberta company doing going international, especially in a country like Colombia?'" he recalls. "All I was doing was making money, because I bought proven producing reserves for 90 cents a barrel in the ground."

His son Steve Jr., a Calgary-based geologist, joined Benson. "I really got to know my elder son by working with him," he says. After selling Benson, he started another junior oil company, Kroes Energy Inc., which was a small partner in a big Cuban offshore play that turned out to be an elephant-sized pool of water. Kroes survived that disaster and continues to operate in Ukraine.

In 2003, Benediktson wrote and published a colourful and entertaining memoir, *Stephan's Story: A Half Century in the International Oil Business.* It begins: "All of my life, I have had this drive to visit and to get to know new places. I have been following that drive since at 17 years of age I hitchhiked up the Alaska Highway to the Yukon Territories." Currently, he is CEO of Daleco Resources Corp., a small publicly traded American resource company based in West Chester, Pennsylvania. The company owns industrial mineral deposits (calcium carbonate, kaolin, and zeolite) in the U.S. Southwest and has interests in producing oil wells in the Appalachians, Texas, and Oklahoma.

Benediktson, who will be 73 this year, lives in the mountain resort of San Miguel de Allende, Mexico, with his second wife Adriana – but he shows no signs of becoming a typical retiree. He has an oil company to run. "We need to get our cash flow up and there's no better way to do this than with oil and gas production, particularly at these prices."

He feels blessed that he's had an eventful life in the international oil business. But none of it would have been possible without two people, he says. The first was his mother, who kept at him to return to school. The other was Charlie Visser , an Imperial Oil drilling superintendent. It took all the courage that Benediktson could muster to phone Visser one day in 1957 and tell him that he had decided to return to school. "He told me, 'Boy, if that's what you'd like to do, go back. I'll give you a leave of absence, and you can come back whenever you can'."

The late 1950s and early 1960s were interesting times to be a student at the University of Alberta, as it turned out. "We had a lot of future leaders and future politicians at the university. [The Right Honourable Mr. Justice] Joe Clark was there, Hon. Harvie Andre (Chemical '62, PhD Chemical '66), Lou Hyndman, and Grant Notley, to name a few. It was a unique experience and one that I am very grateful for," he says.

He also remembers the "exceptional" instructors who taught him engineering. They included dean of engineering Dr. George

Govier (MSc Chemical '45), who was later chair of the Alberta Energy Resources Conservation Board, Leonard Gads (Civil '39), Alan Peterson (Civil '52, MSc Civil '54), Dr. George Ford (Civil '42, MSc Civil '46, DSc [Hon] '88) and a PhD professor a few years younger than Benediktson, the future Dean of Engineering, Peter Adams . Like many engineers who went on to success as entrepreneurs, Benediktson credits his training for giving him an edge. "Some people in the business world are very tunnel-visioned, but in the engineering world you are trained to look at the options and to analyze the situation, whether it's an engineering problem or a business problem," he explains. And in the petroleum industry, engineering and business acumen are going to be in greater demand than ever before. Benediktson accepts M. King Hubbert's projections that world oil production is at its peak during this decade and will steadily decline from here on out.[1] On the upside of the oil supply curve, to get three million barrels of oil a day you had to drill 300 wells in Saudi Arabia. On the downside, it will take a $100 billion investment in the oil sands.

"Capital requirements are endless, limitless. It boggles the mind," Benediktson says. There is also an insatiable demand for engineering talent. "Right now our industry is straining for lack of resources, principally human resources," he explains. During the downturn of the 1980s, fewer students went into geology or petroleum engineering, which now leaves a serious shortage of experienced engineers under 40 years old. "Now, we're over-heated. We're picking over old fields. We're going into coal bed methane. Last week I sat through a presentation where they're

---

[1]M. King Hubbert was a geophysicist who worked for Shell's research lab in Houston, and later at the United States Geological Survey, and as a professor at Stanford and Berkeley. He theorized that oil discovery and production when plotted on a graph would resemble a bell curve. He correctly predicted in the 1950s that U.S. production would peak in the early 1970s. He also predicted that world production would peak around 2000 to 2010. If correct, that means that we are either at "peak oil" or past the peak. It's all downhill from there. Until demand can fall to meet production and discovery, we will be in a permanent state of oil shortage. The same happens to natural gas a decade or two out.

trying to extract natural gas from a shale formation in Arkansas. It's almost unlimited the ways were going to try to have product available to meet market demand."

In an industry where giants dominate, such as Exxon, which made US $9.9 billion in profit in three months last year, Benediktson believes there is room for small players like Daleco, with a market capitalization of $14 million US.

These small fish concentrate on two or three areas where they know the territory and the people. He explains, "They will drill if they have to, but exploration is always risky and there are other ways to grow production." Re-working and re-developing previously uneconomic reservoirs is one such method. Better surface equipment, lifting and injecting water into the reservoir can also increase production.

"All of these things help small companies to reach their production targets at which time they frequently elect to sell out and do it over and over again," he says. As long as there is oil to be coaxed out of the ground, there will be ambitious engineers, Alberta farm boys with wanderlust, and the grandsons of poets willing to give it a try.

"I think it's a wonderful business," says one restless Viking.

Part 1

Some Speeches

Chapter 1

Oil and Gas Experiences

*Delivered at the Icelandic National League: Reyk-
javik, Iceland October 14, 2006 and again in an abridged
version at the University of Akureyri, Iceland, October 19, 2006.*

If you will allow me, I would like to summarize my personal oil
and gas experiences and then go on to talk about the current
status of the industry, as I see it.

I was born and raised on a farm near Markerville, which,
as I am sure you know, was an Icelandic settlement in Central
Alberta. Oil was discovered in the Turner Valley, just south of
Calgary, Alberta, in the 1920s. That discovery led to Western
Canada's first oil boom. However, it was not until 1947, soon
after the Second World War, that Alberta experienced its second oil boom when oil was discovered near Leduc, and over the
next few years, a number of very significant oil fields, Redwater,
Pembina, Joffre, etc. were discovered. A lot of Americans and
American equipment and know-how came to western Canada to
participate in this boom. The American oil industry was firmly
launched soon after the turn of the century by the discovery of
oil at the famous field called Spindletop, near Beaumont, Texas.
The know-how and the equipment and many of those Americans
stayed in Western Canada. At the same time a lot of young men
from the Alberta farms went to work in the oil fields, particularly
on the drilling rigs and in seismic operations, as I did in 1953. I
never did go back to the farm and must say I have never had a
bad year since. I have found the oil business to be a fascinating,
challenging business.

After a number of years working on the drilling rigs, I went
back to school and earned a degree in engineering from the University of Alberta. I took a leave of absence from Esso's drilling

department and after graduation continued working for Esso as an engineer, first in Canada, then in the United States, Australia, Indonesia and Saudi Arabia. Since that time I have worked for the Government of Canada, regulating oil and gas activities in the Arctic; I have consulted to the industry; I have managed a subsidiary of a Fortune 500 American oil company in the United Arab Emirates, a private oil and gas company in Argentina, and for some 14 years I managed a Canadian junior oil and gas company, Benson Petroleum Ltd.

I started Benson on the Alberta venture exchange when I returned to Alberta from Argentina in 1987. Some two years after that start up, I had the good fortune to be joined by my eldest son, Stephan Robert . Steve is an exploration geologist, with at that time some 12 years of diversified experience. Neither of us knew how it would be to work together, but it worked out very well. Since that time, I have, with associates, formed two other junior Canadian oil and gas companies, principally for operating in international oil and gas activities. One operates in the Ukraine. Actually I started it to explore for oil and gas offshore Cuba, but that did not work out. The other company operates principally in South America, Colombia and Brazil, and has been very successful. The Ukraine has been a challenge, but I am still optimistic regarding the potential there.

When we sold Benson Petroleum Ltd. in 2001, I retired to San Miguel de Allende, in the mountains of Central Mexico. Last year I received an unsolicited job offer that I could not resist and I went back to work. I am again active in oil and gas, as well as in mining industrial minerals.

I must say, nevertheless, that over the years the oil and gas industry, like the world, has changed unbelievably. In 1953 when I started working in the oil fields, the world was producing some 28 million barrels of oil per day. Oil sold for $3 per barrel and natural gas for 30 cents per thousand cubic feet. Today the world is consuming some 84 million barrels per day: oil is more or less $60 per barrel and natural gas is more or less $6 per thousand cubic feet.

In 1953, very few farms in Western Canada had either electrical power or natural gas service. 1953 was a banner year for our household in several ways. Early that year my mother received a telegram inviting her to Iceland to unveil the cenotaph to her father, Stephan G. Stephansson , at Sauðárkrókur. This was a major event in the community. To that time very few people in our part of the world had been inside an aeroplane. You can imagine the interest around Markerville when mother left and the questions when she returned. This was 1953, the 100th anniversary of the poet's birth. I often think of what a major event it must have been for the poet when he was invited back to Iceland in 1917. He took the train near Markerville to New York City and then proceeded by ship to Iceland, not an insignificant journey at that time.

In the oil industry, the exploration and drilling for oil is the same as for gas. To minimize our financial risk we do all that is possible, exploration-wise, before we drill (seismic, mapping, etc), but the only way to know if there is oil or gas there is to drill. The results may be oil, gas or water, and through the 50s and 60s oil was the preferred result. Oil could be transported, on trucks if necessary, whereas you needed a pipeline and a market to move natural gas. Throughout the past century, around the world, vast quantities of natural gas, produced in association with oil have been simply burned off, in order to sell the oil. There was little demand for natural gas in the Middle East, certainly no need for heating, and the producers needed massive investments in petrochemical plants to conserve the gas. When I lived in Saudi Arabia in the mid-70s, Aramco produced 10 million barrels of oil per day and flared, that is burned, all of the associated gas, some 3 billion cubic feet per day.

The supply of oil in the ground is not infinite. It is what we call a wasting asset. The global supply-demand situation has been well documented for years, but asking the public to consume less energy has not been a popular position to take politically. Today one of the most serious challenges facing the world is that the supply of oil and gas cannot be expected to continue to meet the demand for oil and gas. The consequences of this are going to be very far reaching, particularly for the

United States, as it is by far the largest consuming nation in the world. Today the United States consumes some 22 million barrels per day while their domestic production has dropped to less than six million barrels per day.

In my opinion, our politicians have left us ill-prepared for the future with respect to our energy needs. In 1956 a well-known and respected earth scientist, M. King Hubbert , accurately predicted the 1970 peak of U.S. oil production. In 1969 he published a curve known as Hubbert's Peak predicting that global production would peak soon after the turn of the century. Another very clever and humorous earth scientist, Kenneth S. Deffeyes , who knew and endorsed King Hubbert's work, has nominated Thanksgiving Day, November 24, 2005, as World Oil Peak Day.

OPEC was formed in 1960 when the crude oil price was $3 per barrel. The Arab Oil Embargo, when Arab nations curtailed production by 5 million barrels per day in response to the US support of Israel during the Yom Kippur War, lasted from October 1973 to March 1974. After the embargo the price of crude oil stood at $12 per barrel and confirmed that the control of crude oil price had passed from the US to OPEC. The time of the embargo gave us a taste of a world with a shortage of crude oil. For example, the US congress passed a law limiting the speed of all traffic to 50 miles per hour to save on fuel. I can recall driving to Kennedy airport during the oil embargo (we lived in Ottawa at that time), taking a flight to Latin America and on our return looking for a place to buy gasoline for the return trip. The queues were long and the tempers were hot. I recall a very large, angry black taxi driver walking by, stopping at our car when he saw the Canadian license plate and (as I hunkered behind the steering wheel) announcing to the crowd, "Look at this guy. He's not even American." Those lessons are long forgotten.

It has been popular for politicians to talk about reducing reliance on imported oil and gas. It has been popular for politicians to talk about developing alternate sources of energy, but the fact is these alternatives are not nearly as convenient or cost effective as oil and gas. The obvious alternate sources of energy are first and foremost coal, a good news – bad news story. The good news is that it is abundant and well-priced; the bad news is that it comes with killer smog, acid rain, hazardous underground mines or surface disturbing open pit mines.

Canada and Venezuela have an abundance of tar sands. Mining the tar sands is a massive materials handling challenge. They are using trucks that haul 400 tons per load, and the process requires enormous quantities of fresh water and natural gas to heat the sands to separate out the oil.

In terms of cost, uranium is an attractive alternate for generating electricity, but since the 1979 melt down at Three Mile Island and the 1986 explosion at Chernobyl, nuclear power has become enormously unpopular. No new nuclear power plants have been built in the United States since 1973.

I had the good fortune to attend the opening of the world's first hydrogen filling station here in Reykjavik in 2003. I was actually in Reykjavik attending a conference commemorating 150 years since Stephan G. Stephansson was born. I believe the jury is still out on whether it takes more energy to supply the hydrogen than you get back when you drive the car. Companies will manufacture hydrogen-powered cars if there are hydrogen filling stations, but who will bear the cost of these service stations?

We have heard a lot about the use of ethyl alcohol from corn as a fuel substitute/additive. Several analysts have computed that producing ethyl alcohol from corn consumes more fossil fuel energy than you get back when you burn the alcohol. It is nonetheless, a popular concept in farm states with subsidies for producing alcohol.

It is interesting to speculate on the changes that may result from the impending oil shortages. First and foremost is the need to reduce the amount of fuel used in passenger cars. We need to change to smaller, more fuel efficient cars, travel less and share the trips. People must use public transport; the short-term solution is to move people by bus, as they do in Latin America. People need to travel less, and so they must live in concentrated areas, closer to their work places, as they do in Europe. The cost of airline travel may be expected to increase. We need to reverse the throw-away society mentally that has dominated America since World War II. The enormous quantities of plastics that are used to package items and are then destroyed each day must be reduced. Plastics are made from hydrocarbons, oil and or gas. We need to use less energy for cooling and heating, less cold air conditioning and before cranking the heater up, put on a sweater. There is a sense of accomplishment in living frugally. All of these things will make a difference. Our life style will depend more and more on conservation rather than consumption.

In the longer term, we will increase the amount of tar sands and coal in use and we will return to constructing nuclear power plants. Humanity will survive and flourish, but with a different set of priorities; you do not need the biggest SUV on the block but the most fuel efficient one.

Recommended Reading

Hartmann, Thom. *The Last Hours of Ancient Sunlight: The Fate of the World and What We Can Do Before It's Too Late.* New York: Broadway Books, 2004.

Deffeyes, Kenneth S. *Beyond Oil: The View from Hubbert's Peak.* New York: Hill and Wang, 2006.

Chapter 2

The Key to Sustainable Energy

Delivered at the Unitarian Universalist Fellowship,
San Miguel de Allende, December 7, 2008.

I left the farm in Central Alberta to go to work in the oil fields
as a teenager in the early 1950s, and I have not had a bad year
since. It is a wonderful, challenging and fascinating business, but
I must admit that I do not always agree with how the industry
is administered. Over forty years ago I did a thesis on population pressures, and since then I have worked as a Petroleum
Engineer and in Executive positions in the industry in USA,
Canada, Australia, the Far East, the Middle East and South
America. I have always advocated conservation over immediate
profits, albeit sometimes with a mixed reception.

I feel strongly that we need to sustain our precious non-
renewable resources, in particular oil and gas, and to protect
the environment and that the key to achieving this is to reduce
consumption. That may be the most effective thing we can do,
but it is not a popular idea, politically or industrially. Reducing
consumption means reducing economic activity not increasing
it, and that has not been an acceptable position. We are always
expected to grow.

In my opinion, North Americans need mass transit systems
in their cities and between their cities. North Americans need to
ride more buses as they do in South America and the Far East.
Last fall I found myself stuck in freeway traffic in New York City,
Atlanta, Los Angeles, Calgary and Mexico City, all within a period of two months. This experience always serves to emphasis
to me how some changes need to be made. In my opinion, people need to start living in concentrated areas near centralized
transportation systems, as they do in Europe and the Far East.
The wide open spaces we enjoy in our cities have to be developed

in a more efficient, concentrated manner. For example, I visit Palm Desert occasionally, which to me is a beautiful city but is a classic example of a spread out city where you have to travel miles by car for whatever you need or whatever you choose to do. A lot of our housing subdivisions do not even have sidewalks, as though the developers never contemplated anything but traveling by car. I have acquaintances who remind me that when gasoline was selling for 35 cents a gallon 40 years ago I used to say it should be $1.00 a gallon in order to reduce consumption.

Petroleum is a wasting asset. It is not being replenished, and after it is consumed it is gone forever. Certainly price is the primary market controller of demand for a commodity, and in the past year we have witnessed a reduction in consumption of gasoline as a result of higher prices. What is remarkable to me is how the political establishments in Canada and the USA are able to continue to avoid the subject, apparently in good conscience. Admittedly it is not a popular subject, but it is a critically important subject for mankind. World-wide production of crude oil is over 80 million barrels per day; the USA consumes over 20 million barrels per day of that while the production of crude oil in the USA is less than 5 million barrels per day. The USA borrows a billion dollars every day to import oil. I have not heard any of our politicians say, "People, we have to stop using so much oil and gas; use smaller cars, ride the bus, live in more concentrated areas." This to me is all fundamental stuff, but obviously it is not a good news story.

In the early 70s I worked in Indonesia. Our oilfields were in Sumatra where there was little demand for natural gas, nobody needed heat and there was very little industrial demand for gas in Sumatra. As result there was no infrastructure for gathering and processing natural gas. Natural gas is always produced in association with oil. We call it solution gas, and in the absence of a system for gathering the gas we would flare and burn it. We would flare and burn a million cubic feet of natural gas a day from a well in order to produce and sell 100 barrels of oil. This was not only a waste of natural gas but the cause of significant carbon dioxide emissions that we have since learned are detrimental to the environment and the probable cause of climate change.

In the mid 70s I worked for Aramco in Saudi Arabia. I was there when Aramco's production peaked at some 11 million barrels of oil per day. At that time all of the solution gas that was produced with the oil in the Kingdom was flared off and burned as Aramco did not have the facilities installed to conserve the gas. We burned or wasted in the order of 3 billion standard cubic feet of natural gas every day in order to supply the world's demand for oil at that time. The desert was lit up for miles, and the flares could be seen for hundreds of miles from the air. At least in significant part, this incredible waste of natural gas resulted in the Saudi Government nationalizing the Saudi Arabian oil reserves and installing the conservation facilities themselves. The original owners, Exxon, Mobil, Chevron and Texaco, continue to operate the oil fields in Saudi Arabia to this day, but since the mid 80s they have been contractors to the Saudi government. Meanwhile the natural gas has since the mid 80s been gathered and processed in a vast petrochemical complex built by the Saudi Government. The enormous quantities of natural gas that were flared and burned with all of the accompanying emissions prior to the mid 80s remains a silent black legacy. I suppose the emissions are still up there someplace.

The Province of Alberta is blessed with vast reserves of heavy oil called oil sands. Low gravity or so called heavy oil is contained in sand on the surface and must essentially be boiled out of the sand. This requires heavy oil processing plants that mine the oil sands and use enormous quantities of natural gas for heating and fresh water for processing to extract the oil. The process became profitable when the price of crude oil reached and exceeded $50 a barrel. Vice President Dick Cheney visited Ft. McMurray a few years ago. The political establishment in Alberta has to date approved over 90 such projects.

The frenzy of activity in the oil sands over the past ten years has disrupted the economy of Alberta and is in danger of destroying the environment over a vast part of North Eastern Alberta. The price of houses in Alberta essentially tripled; the shortage of labor was so acute that some McDonalds who were paying staff $15 per hour had to reduce their service. The infrastructure in the Fort McMurray area was so limited that day labourers were being flown to work, back and forth, morning and night from Edmonton, a distance of some 300 miles. Meanwhile the area is being dotted with enormous lakes of contaminated fresh water and natural gas supplies are being depleted. I am at a total loss to explain the urgency to as we say "go to the bank today". The oil will still be there and will become more valuable as demand is growing while supply is diminishing. Why disrupt the economy and pollute the environment at this pace. Why not approve plants at a sustainable rate?

We hear a lot about alternative energy sources; wind power, solar power, hydrogen cells, ethanol, etc. The fact is that the majority of these alternatives are viable, but at best they will only provide a small fraction of the worlds energy needs. The bio-fuel industry is the most controversial today as the industry is being expanded while the production of bio-fuel is not economically viable. Bio-fuels survive on taxpayer subsidies of some 80 billion dollars to corn growers. The six largest public companies in the business have lost more than 8.7 billion dollars in the past three years and the bio-fuel industry is being blamed for soaring food costs. This is another energy issue being manipulated by political not economic motives. I would draw your attention to an article on the subject in the *Financial Times* of October 23rd.

The practical proven, sustainable energy alternatives today are nuclear power plants and that tried and true fossil fuel, coal. I understand there are over 13 new reactors being built or are planned for in the USA today. Global reserves of coal are sufficient to meet the worlds energy needs for several generations, although a lot of work needs to be done to protect the environment from the effects of commercializing coal reserves.

I would like to give you an overview of one positive story of sustainable energy that underlines mankind's ingenuity in essentially any field of endeavour. This story is about how the country of Iceland uses renewable energy sources, hydroelectric and geothermal, to provide 70% of its primary energy needs.

11

Iceland is located in one of the most tectonically active parts of the world. There are over 200 volcanoes and over 600 hot springs located in the country. Iceland has harnessed geothermal energy since 1907. The capital city of Reykjavík, sometimes called the chimneyless city, has been served by geothermal heat via a pipeline connection since 1930. Iceland has pioneered geothermal engineering, and courses in geothermal engineering attract an international student body to Iceland each year under the auspices of the United Nations. Geothermal energy is not feasible everywhere, but modern technology allows its use in places not previously considered feasible.

Hydropower is harnessed in Iceland through its abundant supply of glacial rivers and waterfalls. The supply of electrical power, from both hydro and geothermal plants, has resulted in significant industrialization in Iceland. For example, they refine aluminum from bauxite ore, an electro chemical process that uses a lot of electrical power. Iceland has an abundance of electrical power and deep water ports, and this combination has led to the importation of bauxite ore for refining. The first bauxite refinery was commissioned in Iceland in 1968. Coincidentally I attended the inauguration celebrations in Reykjavik of that refinery. One additional bauxite refinery is currently under construction and a third is planned.

As a natural extension of Iceland's focus on renewable energy supplies and in part driven by a desire to avoid the high cost of importing oil, Iceland began testing the use of hydrogen as a fuel source. A Professor at the University of Iceland originally proposed the idea of using hydrogen as a fuel source during the oil embargo in 1973. In 2001 three fuel cell buses built by Daimler Chrysler were commissioned in Reykjavík, followed by a hydrogen fuelling station commissioned by Shell in 2003. I coincidentally attended the inauguration of that hydrogen fuelling station. This test, the first commercial operating test of public transportation powered by hydrogen fuel cells in the world, operated successfully until 2005. A significant benefit of the use of hydrogen fuel cells is that carbon dioxide emissions are kept to a minimum.

The last century, the 20th, was a century of development. The world enjoyed all manner of developments from cars to computers. Since the 1980s we have consumed more than we produce, making up the difference by borrowing. As we move ahead in the new century, the 21st, it appears this may become a century of consolidation, adjusting for the excesses of the past century, as well as a century of survival. It would appear we are facing global shortages of food, water and various commodities, including petroleum. We can only hope that mankind's creativity will rise to the challenges and generate and provide the solutions necessary for us to continue to enjoy the lifestyle we have become accustomed to.

Chapter 3

Why is the USA Addicted to Oil?

Delivered at a Panel Discussion for the Center for Global Justice, San Miguel de Allende, Mexico, August 4, 2009.

It gives me a great deal of pleasure to be asked to join this panel today. I particularly like talking about the oil business. I went to work in the oil fields as a teenager in the early 50s, and since then I have lived and worked as a Petroleum Engineer or as an Oil Company Executive in the US, Canada, Australia, Indonesia, Saudi Arabia, the United Arab Emirates, Argentina, Colombia and Mexico. It is a wonderful, fascinating business full of challenges.

The reason the US is so addicted to oil is basically because there are 265 million automobiles in the US. In comparison, there are 65 million automobiles in China, which has four times the population. Petroleum is a wasting asset. It is not being replenished, and when it is consumed it is gone forever. Price is the primary free market controller of demand for any commodity, and in the past year we have witnessed a reduction in consumption of gasoline as a result of higher prices. That is good; however, consider the magnitude of this problem. Worldwide crude oil production is over 80 million barrels per day, more or less at a maximum. The US consumes over 20 million barrels of that. Meanwhile crude oil production in the US is now in the order of 5 million barrels per day. The US borrows a billion dollars every day to import oil and gas. Nevertheless, I have not heard any of our politicians say, "People, we have to stop using so much oil and gas; buy smaller cars, ride the bus, live in more concentrated areas." Have you?

Reducing consumption means reducing economic activity, not increasing it, and zero growth has not been an acceptable position in our societies. We are always expected to grow. As a result, since the 80s we have been consuming more than we produce and financing the difference. We have lost sight of the fact that it is the consumer who pays, whether it is for corporate bonuses or for the basic production costs.

Oil and gas reserves everywhere are in an advanced stage of depletion. The reserves discovered in Alberta 60 years ago, the reserves that were put on stream in Australia 40 years ago, the North Slope reserves in Alaska, and the major reserves in the Middle East are all in advanced stages of depletion. Through the years, estimates of the global supplies of oil and gas have been made by governments and oil companies. As far back as 1956 a highly respected earth scientist, M. King Hubbert , accurately predicted the peak of US production which occurred in 1970. Hubert went on to publish a curve known as Hubbert's Peak, predicting that global production would peak soon after the turn of the century. Another very clever earth scientist, Kenneth S. Deffeyes , wrote a book called *Beyond Oil* that agrees with Hubbert and nominated Thanksgiving Day, November 24, 2005 as World Peak Oil Day. I mention this because it never fails to disappoint me that our politicians, whether they have a PhD in Earth Sciences or were pig farmers from Iowa or Saskatchewan, have had access to all of this information on world oil supplies, but they have never addressed the problem.

The US addiction to oil extends beyond our gasoline needs. The amount of plastics used for packaging could be very significantly reduced. All the energy used for heating and air conditioning can be significantly reduced as costs dictate in the future. We can easily learn to live with the thermostats a couple of notches lower by wearing sweaters in the house in the winter time and in the summer time to open the windows or use fans for cooling just as our grandparents did.

A major challenge today is to try to ensure that there will be enough energy available to supply the needs of future generations. I spent a few years with the Federal Government in Canada, which gave me some insight into how governments operate. In my opinion the problem is in large part a result of our democratic form of government. Democracy, founded over a thousand years ago when the Chieftains in Iceland used to meet at the Althing each year to sort out their country's problems, is certainly the best form of government we have been able to come up with to date, but it is not perfect.

It seems obvious to me that there was very little or no long term planning in government. Our politicians have a four year shelf life, and their major issue is to get re-elected. It is a lot more fun to be in power than in the opposition. Putting forward solutions for the long term supply of energy and water is probably not going to help a politician get re-elected. Yet these issues are very important, too important to be left entirely to our politicians operating in a four year time frame. Perhaps we need a sort of Super Committee of Experts, removed from politics, to recommend publicly our country's policy on critical issues such as energy. There needs to be some regulation of resources such as oil and water to ensure future supplies.

For the last century we have lived in a throw-away society of conspicuous consumption. In this new century we must become increasingly more frugal, and the conservation of our wasting assets must become increasingly more acceptable. I believe that a lot of unpopular measures such as actively campaigning for oil conservation, less air conditioning and heat, less packaging and a lower speed limit should be implemented.

I leave you with these thoughts.

Chapter 4

The Icelandic Economy

Delivered at the Center for Global Justice, San Miguel
de Allende, Mexico, March 27, 2013.

Honoured Guests, Ladies and Gentlemen,

I feel obliged to give you a little background on Iceland that you understandably might not know. The country was settled around 870 by Norwegians, and at this time there are some 320,000 people living in Iceland. I love being part of a minority group. At that time the Norwegian King Haraldur, known as Haraldur Fairhair, was confiscating their property and charging too much tax, etc. When they left they did not want anyone to follow them, particularly Haraldur, so they called the country Iceland. A few years later they set up a colony where they wanted people to follow them, so they called it Greenland.

The Icelanders have the oldest democracy in the world; the Chieftains would meet once a year at Þingvellir to settle disputes and make laws and so on. The year 1,000 was noteworthy for two reasons: first, at the annual meeting they agreed to convert to Christianity, they were pagans to that time; and second, a born-in-Iceland, Icelander, Leifur Eríksson, discovered America and established a settlement there. The Icelanders needed a connection to Europe, so after some 200 years they voluntarily went under the Norwegian crown. Unfortunately, some 400 years later, Norway and Denmark had a war and Denmark won, so the Icelanders became a colony of Denmark. The Danes abused this connection for commercial reasons; you had to "buy everything in the company store," so as to speak, so during World War II, when Denmark was occupied by the Germans, the Icelanders sent them a telegram, which I have read. These are my words, but the telegram in effect said, "It's been a great ride, but we're out of here. We are now a republic."

In the 1870s, one third of the population of Iceland emigrated in search of a better life, and most of those émigrés went to America. Icelanders still call it the New World over here. All four of my grandparents left at that time; my mother's parents homesteaded first in Wisconsin in 1873, then North Dakota in 1880, then in Alberta in 1889. Curiously, Icelanders are very academic; they have the most book stores per capita and a high level of education. I once read a report by an Englishman who toured Iceland in the late 1800s and again in my words he said something like, "What kind of people are these. I go to a humble farm in the North of Iceland and find the farmer reading Homer or the Bible or something like this."

Unveiling of Stephan G. Stephansson Cenotaph
Markerville, Alberta – September 4, 1950

My strong Icelandic connection is because my mother's father, Stephan G. Stephansson, in addition to all of this homesteading on the frontier, fathering eight children, doing a lot of community work and so on, wrote over 2,000 pages of poetry and most remarkably was recognized in his time for his philosophy and literary talent.

Stephan G., as he is known, was essentially the poet laureate of Iceland while living in Canada. He is still taught in the schools in Iceland, and as a result the Presidents of Iceland generally visit Alberta to pay homage to Stephan G.; his farm home is an Alberta Heritage Site, and there are monuments to him at his gravesite, at Markerville, Alberta, at Gardar, North Dakota and at his birth place in Northern Iceland.

Before I retired to Mexico, I was the Honorary Consul of Iceland in Alberta, and I have met all but one of Iceland's Presidents and a few of the Prime Ministers. As a point of interest, Iceland had the first democratically elected female Head of State, Her Excellency Vigdís Finnbogadóttir, whom I have met.

I could go on about this fascinating, beautiful country, but will instead recommend three articles here to twig your interest: "Best Place to Live", *Reuters*, November 2007; "Happiest People", *The Observer*, John Carlin, May 2008; and "Renewable Energy", *Wikipedia*.

Now, on to the Icelandic Economy. For years Iceland was the poorest country in Europe. The economy was largely driven by fishing and has today also added tourism. Iceland was responsible for the extension of "territorial waters" from 10 miles to 200 miles some 40 years ago. The Icelanders would get up in the morning and see British, Portuguese, or Japanese cannery boats sucking up their cod fish stocks, just off the coast line. No one, not the United Nations, the World Court, the European Union or NATO, seemed to pay any attention to their objections. Iceland has no military. They do have a few policemen, but they do not carry fire arms. To get international attention, the Icelanders started cutting their net lines and ramming these foreign cannery boats with their tug boats, and in due course were able to realize the extension of territorial waters to 200 miles.

The Icelanders had three significant banks: Glitnir, Landsbanki and Kaupthing, when they deregulated banking in 2001. In 2003 Iceland's banks were privatized, and they promptly uploaded their debt, principally in Europe, and in some very creative ways. Iceland became one of the richest countries in the world. Icesave, Landsbanki's brand name in the UK and the Netherlands, offered online banking whose minimal costs allowed them to pay relatively high rates of return. The owner of Landsbanki, Björgólfur Guðmundsson, acquired the ultimate toy of the rich and famous, a soccer team: West Ham United. I had the pleasure of joining Björgólfur in Toronto in 2007 when West Ham toured the New World.

As the banks' foreign investments grew so did their foreign debt; in 2003 Iceland's foreign debt was 200 times GNP and in 2007 it was 900 times. In 2008, the three big banks went bankrupt and were nationalized; there is a detailed record of this crisis in *Wikipedia*. Contrary to what could be expected, the crisis resulted in Iceland recovering their sovereign rights, through a process of direct participatory democracy that eventually led to a new Constitution. Protests and riots eventually forced the government of Prime Minister Geir Haarde to resign, and in September 2008 the Parliament of Iceland voted to indict Haarde on charges of negligence in office. His integrity in terms of taking bribes or otherwise profiting was never in question. Haarde received a suspended sentence, but it is my understanding that he spent a little time in jail, which must have been a humbling experience. I am told that Iceland's jails have never been upgraded as they are only occasionally used for things like over-nighting drunks. Several former bank officials, politicians and government employees were charged, some were convicted, and some were imprisoned.

In March 2009, a new Prime Minister, Jóhanna Sigurðardóttir was sworn in and has since presided over a coalition government. We spent April 2012 in Iceland, during which time I was invited for lunch in the Parliamentary Cafeteria by a Member of Parliament. During the lunch, I looked over and saw a lady that looked vaguely familiar. When I asked Össur, "Who is that lady," he looked over and called out; "Jóhanna, come here." She came over and we had a very pleasant chat.

What happened after Jóhanna was sworn in was extraordinary. The previous government had agreed that Icelanders would pay off a total of three and a half million Euros with interest of 5.5%, which would have required each Icelandic citizen to pay about $130 per month for 15 years to settle a debt incurred by private parties. The President, Ólafur Ragnar Grímsson, refused to ratify a law that would have made Icelands citizens responsible for its bankers' debts and called for a referendum.

I was reminded of a conversation I had with Ólafur Ragnar in 2009. I had taken my daughter, Susan Rosa Abbiati Benediktson,[1] my two granddaughters, Sofia and Delfina, and my youngest son, Paul David Benediktson, to visit to visit Iceland, and Ólafur Ragnar had invited us for tea and cookies at Bessastaðir, the Presidential residence. I was determined to ask him about the crisis, so when I had chance I told him how I had lived through two such economic crises in Argentina. I told him (he did not ask for my opinion) that if I had such a problem I would do three things: first, I would engage a negotiator, preferably an Argentine with World Bank experience; second, I would drag it out as long as possible, since time works wonders; third, I would negotiate the "haircut" – the haircut became an everyday term in the Buenos Aires press and generally finished in the Argentine case at more or less 70% of the book value of the debt. Olafur Ragnar said, "Oh no, we could not do that."

The international community increased the pressure on Iceland, particularly the UK and the Netherlands. They threatened dire reprisals such as blocking aid from the IMF, freezing the savings and checking accounts of Icelanders, and so on. In the referendum held in March, 2010, 93% of the Icelanders voted against repayment of the debt. Iceland's social, nonviolent revolution (never televised in the United States) was not over, however. The Icelanders decided to prepare a new constitution, updated for today's realities, free from the undue influence of international finance and money. The people of Iceland elected twenty five adults from a group of 522 citizens; each individual was put forward by at least thirty citizens, to write the new constitution on the internet. The group selected included students, journalists, farmers, trade union representatives and lawyers, all without political party affiliations. Citizens could witness the

---

[1]Susan attended the American College in Switzerland, the University of Calgary and has a Masters degree in Merchandising from the Fashion Institute of Technology in Manhattan.

David, Susan, Stephan, President Grimsson, Sofia and Delfina
Bessastaðir, The Presidential Residence, April 2009

development of the document and could send their comments and suggestions in a democratic process, before it was sent to parliament for approval. Unfortunately, the constitution was rejected in parliament.

Part 2

Oil Patch Tales

Chapter 5

Bennett and Hurst

After harvest on the farm near Markerville in the fall of 1953, I decided to look for a job in the oilfields, just for the winter. The Sigurdson boys had gone to work for a slim-hole drilling company called Bennett and Hurst, so I went into Red Deer and found their office. Bill Hurst hired me on the spot. As it turned out, I have yet to return to full time farming. The Hursts were a Master Farm family from Nanton, Alberta, and George Bennett was always noted as having married a Harper of Calgary's Harper Tire store. Bill looked after operations and George the administration and contracts from an office in Calgary. Our major client was Chevron, and our major competitor was Seaman Brothers, known as "those guys from Saskatchewan".

The Bennett and Hurst company owned two slim-hole rigs, a Failing 1500 and a Mayhew. The pay was 90 cents an hour, no overtime pay back then, and the pace was quite hectic. Bennett and Hurst were then notable for having carried out Western Canada's first offshore drilling operation. The year before, on contract to Chevron, they had mounted a slim-hole drilling rig on a barge on Gull Lake and drilled slim holes until a storm upset the barge and they lost the rig into the lake.

That fall we drilled around Pine Lake, then Nanton, and after freeze up we drilled in the Harmon Valley east of Peace River. We lived in one big room over Joe Gault's garage in Nampa. Joe filled the big room above his garage with double bunk beds, put a bathroom and shower at one end, and charged us $2 per day. We ate at the local restaurant, because it was the only place to eat in town and because they had an attractive young waitress, Stella.

24

Bennett and Hurst slim-hole rig and water truck
Harman Valley, 1953

We worked three shifts, three man crews, and rotated shifts each week. There were no days off, but when you changed from the graveyard shift at 8 a.m. you got 30 hours off until the afternoon shift at 4 p.m. the next day, known as a "long change." This was our opportunity to visit the bright lights of Peace River circa 1954.

In the winter slim-hole rigs were fitted with tent covers, which provided a bit of shelter from the cold. Each rig was issued a diesel burning orchard heater. The heaters smoked a lot, and after eight hours near the heater under the tent your face would be black.

One night Curly Hale's glove froze to the kelly bushing as the driller was lowering it into the rotary table and Curly lost the end of his index finger. On the long drive to the hospital in Peace River, Curly worked his way through most of a bottle of whiskey someone came up with as a pain killer. Always a light hearted spirit, by the time he arrived at the hospital he was in a playful mood with the nurses who were taken back by this blackened fellow missing the end of his finger. Later, Curly would delight in holding the stump of his finger to his nose, particularly in a beer parlour, to see the expressions on the patrons' faces as this fellow apparently shoved a couple of inches of finger into his nose.

Chapter 6

Drilling Contractors

In the summer of 1954, the seismic drilling company, Bennett and Hurst won a contract from Shell Oil to drill shot holes for a Shell seismic party in the muskeg area northwest of White-court. At that time the road north ended at the river at White-court. The bridges and road were yet to be built; all road traf-fic north went through Athabasca. We used Bombardier track-mounted seismic drills with track-mounted water tanks to ser-vice the drilling operation, and the crews lived in a tent camp. The operation was a challenging experience, not to mention the mosquitoes. The operation was a success, but as they say, the patient died. The Bennett and Hurst Drilling Company disap-peared into the annals of the Alberta oilfields soon after that.

I joined two friends who had gone to work on a "big rig" owned by the Canbridge Drilling Company in the prairies around Hanna, Pollockville, Steveville, etc. They paid $1.50 per hour, still no over time. The Canbridge operations schedule was a little different. The owners had brought rigs up from the US and followed the traditional system there. The senior (stud) driller worked day shift, next driller in line worked the afternoon shift and the "green" driller got the graveyard shift; no long changes. I worked for the afternoon driller. The rig was a Franks rig. You worked as long as the rig had a contract, no days off except when the rig could not be moved during road bans in the spring. During the rig moves we all worked day shift. Our occasional visits to the beer parlours in those prairie towns usually ended up with one of the drillers fighting with one of the cowboys.

The big rigs particularly liked the farm boys; they didn't ask why, they just did it. It was hard to find a place to live in these

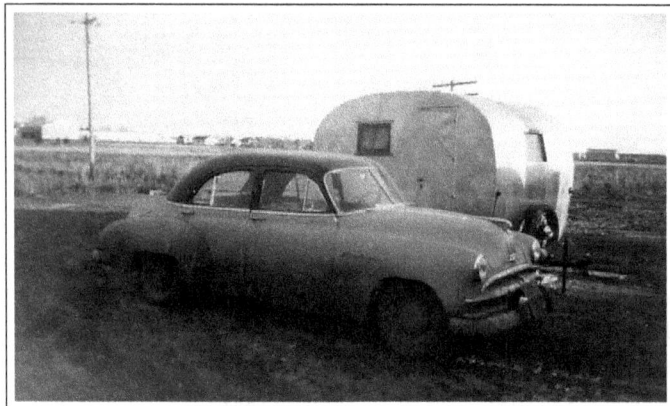

A place to sleep while rough-necking on the prairies in the fifties.

old prairie ghost towns, so I bought a small old trailer that I could pull behind my car. A friend, Neil McQuaig, lived with me. Neil worked for the green driller and one day when they came on shift at midnight Neil confessed, "I went into Hanna today and had a few beers, came home and put a steak on the stove and fell asleep. The steak burned and things smell a little from that." The trailer smelled of burnt meat until I sold it.

I damaged a few of my fingers and had to take some time off at home. There I discovered we were having an oil boom in the Joffre field just east of Red Deer, so I switched to Parker Drilling, closer to home. These rigs had also been brought up from the US. Parker was probably the roughest drilling contractor in The Patch. For whatever reason, the rig, a National 55, operated for a few days without the cover on the rotary chain. It was like working beside a crocodile. One day we arrived on the lease and couldn't quite make out what was happening. Someone forgot to pin the pipe rack and it fell to the ground with a full rack of pipe on it. The triple stands of drill pipe were splayed out from the rig like strands of spaghetti. The crew were pulling the stands of drill pipe in towards the rig with the cat line and latching onto them with the elevators.

Chapter 7

Imperial's Rigs

Through the 1950s and beyond, Imperial Oil Limited owned and operated drilling rigs. They employed six full crews of men and a transportation department. Imperial gave days off, paid $2.25 an hour starting wage, overtime and double time on statutory holidays, a shift differential, annual vacations and transported you to the rig back and forth in a shift truck: unbelievable. I had the very good fortune of being hired by their drilling department in January, 1955.

The core staffs of Imperial Oil's Drilling Department were all from the Turner Valley. It seemed as though you didn't rate unless you had worked in "The Valley". It was what the Americans affectionately called a "brother-in-law outfit". The tool pushers included two Jacksons, Joe and George. I worked on George Jackson's rig. Another rig was pushed by Johnny Visser, whose brother Charlie Visser was the Drilling Superintendent. Another rig was pushed by "Ginty" Woolridge, their brother-in-law. We had two Archibalds and two or three McIntyres. The transportation had three Georges, "Red," Bill and Fred. In spite of this, or because of this, it all worked very well and was a great experience.

Imperial had ten or twelve rigs for the six crews, so they could move a rig into any of Canada's well known muskeg areas of the north with no roads. They would build a winter road after freeze up, move the rig in, rig up and drill until the well was finished. The operation was serviced by company aircraft, de Havilland Otters and Beavers. They would move the rig out after freeze up the following winter. We worked six weeks on and two weeks off. The camps were good and the cooking outstanding. Imperial

29

maintained an operations center at Dawson Creek.

The winter of 1954 we drilled a well at Kahntah River. Several of Imperial's big rigs had so-called conventional derricks, (as did our rig, Wilson 2), which were bolted together piece by piece. To rig-up you brought in a rig building crew who bolted the derrick together. The last rig builders, a lost art, were Bill Fry's and McAulder's crews, both out of Turner Valley, of course. Bill Fry brought his crew in to rig us up at Kahntah River. It was something to behold these fellows bolting the structure together, working their way up in the freezing cold, particularly an old man with a bad leg named Swede Olson: scary. The derrick for Wilson 2 now welcomes you as you enter Edmonton from the south.

Chapter 8

Norman Wells

I worked on Imperial Oil's rigs for a number of years. Many of the men in Imperial's Drilling Department were from Turner Valley, where western Canada's oil boom of the 1920s through 1930s happened. It was a great experience. A lot of the men chewed tobacco, because you could not smoke on the rigs. Profanity was an art form. Our tool pusher, George Jackson, was a master of both. If it rained hard, it was "coming down like a cow pissing on a flat rock." If it was noisy, it was "like two skeletons humping on a tin roof in a hail storm."

In 1956 we spent the summer drilling four wells at Norman Wells on the Mackenzie River. The explorer Mackenzie noted the oil seeps in 1789, and in 1919 Imperial Oil sent a six man team, including the geologist Ted Link, an old drilling rig and an ox named Old Nig to pull things up to Norman Wells on a wood burning barge. They landed on the river bank at Norman Wells and while Link did surface geology and some mapping, the men rigged up the rig, drilled ahead and discovered oil at 900 feet. The rest is history. During the following winter they ate Old Nig.

During World War II the Americans were rightfully concerned with national security from the Japanese threat. They constructed the Alaska Highway from Dawson Creek to Fairbanks and the CANOL Project (Canadian American Northern Oil Lines), which included drilling 60 wells at Norman Wells, constructing a pipeline to Whitehorse, and building a refinery there. This was a major project. After the war, Imperial supplied the communities along the Mackenzie with fuel from Norman Wells by barge. As demand increased it became necessary to increase oil production. The majority of the oilfield is under the river. The McKenzie is several miles across at Norman Wells. The east side of the river is called "the mainland."

We drilled two vertical wells without incident. The second two we drilled directionally under the river, deviated 60 degrees from the vertical, the highest angle hole that directional drillers Eastman had drilled to that time. It was not without incident; we got stuck in the hole and did the usual – back-off, run jars and try to jar the fish loose. We wanted to salvage the hole, so we washed over and tried to back off the drill collars by torqueing them up backwards and running string shots, but were unsuccessful. We brought the experts, McCullough Oil Tools up to Norman Wells to help. Then our big boss, Charlie Visser, came up. After watching us trying to back off the drill collars, Charlie told the McCullough man, Abe Weissenborn, "Boy, run a big string shot, not just those fire crackers." Abe ran a shot that got the job done. In fact when the drill collars reached the surface we found they were split from top to bottom.

Chapter 9

Peace River Bridge

In 1957 we were drilling a well at Blueberry, just off the Alaska Highway west of Ft. St. John. To get back to the rig after days off we would fly to Dawson Creek, and the company shift truck would drive us out to the rig. When we got to the Peace River Bridge, to our surprise we found our tool push, George Jackson, waiting for us in a motor boat. The bridge had collapsed the day before.

The Peace is a big river. During World War II the American army had built the Alaska Highway, from Dawson Creek, Mile 0 to Fairbanks, Mile 1450. At the Peace River they had constructed an enormous, beautiful, suspension bridge, anchored at each end by a very large block of concrete. In the interim, Pacific Petroleum had built a plant to process their abundance of natural gas at the crossing. In those years, Imperial Oil had a joint exploration program with Pacific. We were led to believe that more or less any oil found was for Imperial, while any gas would be for Pacific. Imperial was an oil company, and natural gas at 25 cents an mcf (1,000 cubic feet) without pipeline connections was an inconvenience. It turned out that the discoveries seemed to be all gas.

Pacific's water supply for the plant was pumped from the river, and the water line passed in front of the large concrete anchor block on the north side of the river. We were told that during the night the water line had broken and the pump washed the fill out from in front of the bridge's anchor block, allowing it to slide forward. The result was awesome; the two enormous pillars in the river started leaning south. The vertical cables holding the deck of the bridge snapped and wound themselves

The Peace River Bridge
Ft. St. John, B.C., Spring 1957

around the main suspension cables when they broke, and the decks were hanging down to the water.

Chapter 10

Brazeau

In 1959 I worked on Ginty Woolridge's rig in the Brazeau, my last full time rough-necking job. There were no roads through that area in those years, so Imperial had typically moved the rig in over a winter road, built an airstrip, and planned on drilling until they finished the well. They would then rack the rig and move it out the next winter. The planners didn't anticipate any problems, so we had just enough fuel and drilling mud. The rig was a brand new National 110. Ginty was a master builder and enjoyed rigging it up in fine style. He told me the rig cost over a million dollars.

One beautiful summer day we drilled down and went to make a connection. When we backed off the drill pipe we realized the well had gone on vacuum, a lost circulation problem. The pattern continued as we went to drill ahead and became stuck in the hole. The next thing that usually happened was that the well began to "kick," to blow out. We closed the blowout preventers and there we sat, the pipe stuck in the hole, unable to circulate drilling mud and the well kicking.

In due course, we solved the lost circulation problem, but in so doing so we ran out of drilling mud materials and were still stuck in the hole. We then initiated an airlift program with Imperial's two Otters flying drilling mud in from the airstrip at Lodgepole. These were not twin Otters but the original single engine Otters, with weight limitations. As time went on, we ran out of diesel fuel and had to install aluminum tanks in the Otters and airlift fuel to the rig. The Otters flew from daylight to dark to keep us going.

We could not solve the stuck problem so we had to back

off and leave all our drill collars in the hole. The question then became how to transport replacement drill collars in to the rig. They were too long and heavy to airlift. The decision was made to bring them in with the Muskox. Imperial had various research projects underway through the years, including Alex Hemstock's project of developing an off-road vehicle for muskeg terrain. They had gone so far as to build a proto-type, the Muskox, the predecessor to the Nodwell. This would be the acid test.

To their very great credit, the crew made it. In due course the Muskox arrived, pulling an Athey wagon carrying our replacement drill collars. I have never before or since seen such an exhausted, mosquito bitten, mud covered group of men as the crew that delivered our drill collars.

Chapter 11

Redwater

In an oil boom as in a war the natural leaders emerge. Working for drilling contractors I worked for young drillers like Heinz Kummer, a farm boy from Barrhead who was twenty years old and had been on the rigs for only two years, drilling oil wells no problem. Working on Imperial's rigs was a bit different because there was no turnover. Men retired, and occasionally someone would quit to return to the farm or work for a service company so they could be home at nights.

I was a high school dropout during my rough-necking years. I had gone to school in Red Deer until just after my 14th birthday in 1947 and had finished grade 10. I went back on leave of absence from Imperial's Drilling Department and graduated in 1958, married with one son. That must be a record of sorts, 11 years to get through high school. I graduated from the University of Alberta in Engineering in 1962. None of this would have been possible without the unwavering support of my first wife, Audrey, a lovely uncomplaining lady, mother of my three fine children.

I greatly appreciated the opportunity to attend the University of Alberta and accordingly made a donation to their new school of Engineering Safety and Risk Management in 2015. The engineering department, in turn, named one meeting room in their new building, the Donadeo Innovation Centre for Engineering, the Stephan V. Benediktson Meeting Room and another one the Rosa Stephansson-Benediktson Meeting Room.

At that time Imperial had an extensive training program, supplemented with courses and training assignments at Esso Production Research Corporation in Houston. They would hire engineers of their choosing from essentially any discipline and train them as petroleum engineers. In my case I graduated with a degree in Civil Engineering and, as a result of Esso's extensive training program, I worked as a Petroleum Engineer throughout my professional years. I have been a member of the Society of Petroleum Engineers (SPE) since 1976 and was a charter director of the SPE branch in the United Arab Emirates. As a measure of my appreciation for this, I have funded the SPE Stephan V. Benediktson Scholarship for third year Canadian Petroleum Engineering students, at any Canadian or USA engineering school.

Imperial ran me through their training program and assigned me to Redwater as the District Production Engineer – great experience. Redwater, a big carbonate reef, was discovered with the series of discoveries following Leduc in 1947. It was one of Alberta's few "elephants," over a billion barrels recoverable, pretty well empty today.

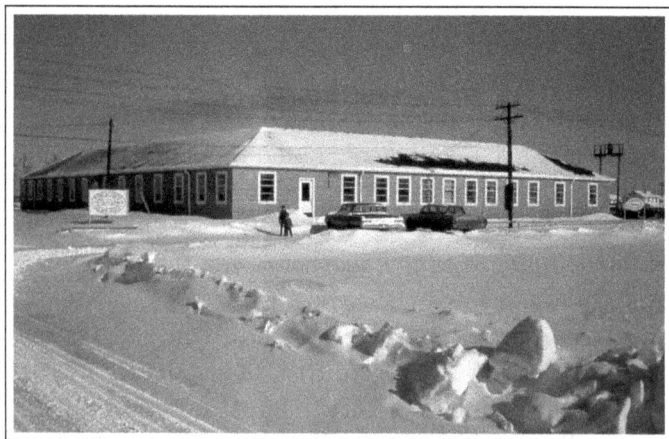

Imperial Oil Limited's offices, Stevie and Susan in foreground
Redwater, Alberta, 1964

Back in those times Canada had productive capacity in excess of market demand, and the wells in each oil field were assigned a production allowable each month, a major function of the ERCB. Allowable production was not transferable, so if a well could not make its allowable that part of the market share was lost.

Imperial had more or less 500 wells in the Redwater field; edge wells, etc. could not always make their allowable. Work-overs to increase production from these marginal wells were an excellent investment opportunity. We had two work-over rigs under contract, and I wrote and supervised more or less one hundred work-over programs per year.

Even then, Redwater showed signs of, and the locals told stories of, the boom years when the field was drilled up and put on production. The area had been largely settled by Ukrainian immigrants, and until that time language was still a problem with some of the older farmers. We heard stories of farmers holding off the trucks from entering with rifles.

The local general store operator, Mike, ran monthly accounts for most people; there were no credit cards in those days. They would deliver as necessary. Mike did well and bought a new Cadillac while we were there, but he never took it out during the day. He knew that if people saw him with a new Cadillac some of them wouldn't pay their bills.

Chapter 12

EPRCo

The industry wisdom in the late 1950s through the mid 1960s was that Canada should maintain a 20 year supply of conventional oil for national security. Export licenses were carefully considered by the National Energy Board. That wisdom has long gone by the boards, replaced with a "Let's go to the bank today" ethic. The last time I checked I believe we are down to about at a six year supply of conventional reserves. Government spending to market Alberta's oil production has always amused me. It is generally accepted that, since the turn of the century, world oil production is on the decline side of the curve. Our neighbour to the south consumes more or less 20 million barrels of oil per day, and their domestic production has declined to more or less five million barrels per day. What's to market?

We spent 1965 in Houston at Esso Production Research Corporation (EPRCo): a great experience. Arriving from Redwater, this was a major cultural adjustment and a growth experience. I spent most of my time working on hydraulic fracturing applications and field testing and assisted in organizing and teaching a Production Engineering School. The exposure to this substantial research facility and the staff was very worthwhile. I had the opportunity to tour the operations of Humble Oil (an Esso affiliate) on the King Ranch, their flagship operation. Humble had leased the oil rights for the whole ranch. Down the hall a few offices was a new recruit – a big PhD engineer from South Dakota, Lee Raymond – who went on to become the CEO of Exxon for probably 15 years and retired a few years ago with a highly publicized $400 million severance payment.

In the 1950s I discovered M. King Hubbert's work on world

oil supply; he correctly predicted that US production would peak in the early 1970s and that world oil production would peak around the years 2000 to 2010. Much of the development of the production of offshore oil and gas reserves was pioneered in the Gulf of Mexico (GOM). We were told at that time that Exxon recognized the industry was going to have to move ever farther out into the offshore margins to meet world demand. To that end, EPRCo would coordinate offshore developments for the affiliates. We needed to prepare for this. I was invited to the christening of the Glomar Conception at a ship yard in Louisiana, my first offshore rig tour. Esso Australia had made a discovery in the Bass Strait, and the North Sea looked like it had potential. The famous London fogs and "grey" London to that time was largely a result of air pollution from burning coal. A supply of natural gas from the North Sea would lead to incredible changes for the Brits as they converted to cleaner burning natural gas; they could see the sun, clean the exterior of their buildings and have them stay clean.

Chapter 13

Australia

In September, 1967 I transferred to Esso Eastern and went to work for the Australian affiliate in Melbourne. Esso had farmed in on BHP's leases in the Bass Straits; it was a 50:50 deal with an override to Lewis Weeks who put the deal together. BHP Oil and Gas, then consisting of some six employees at their head office in Melbourne, had ran seismic over the blocks and found a series of very interesting structures. Esso drilled the structures with a Global Marine drill ship, the Glomar 2, chalking up two oil discoveries, Halibut and Snapper, and two gas discoveries, Barracuda and Marlin. Following a difficult and prolonged negotiation with respect to the oil price (the world was awash in crude oil at that time), they had struck a price of $4.80 per barrel and were now ready to move ahead with the development. To this end Esso recruited various people from the affiliates, and I had the good fortune to make that list.

I was part of a small group of engineers in Melbourne that carried out some world class developments and set a number of records in off-shore developments. The development included five platforms: a ten well platform at Barracuda, a 24 well platform at Marlin, a 24 well platform at Halibut and two 21 well platforms at Snapper.

I was the Marlin Project Engineer. John Gray, my predecessor at Redwater, was the Barracuda Project Engineer, and John Buchannan was the Halibut-Snapper Project Engineer. All platforms were designed by Esso, fabricated and launched at Barry's Beach, Victoria.

The Bass Strait is a very rough body of water with a water depth of some 250 feet in the development area. The platforms

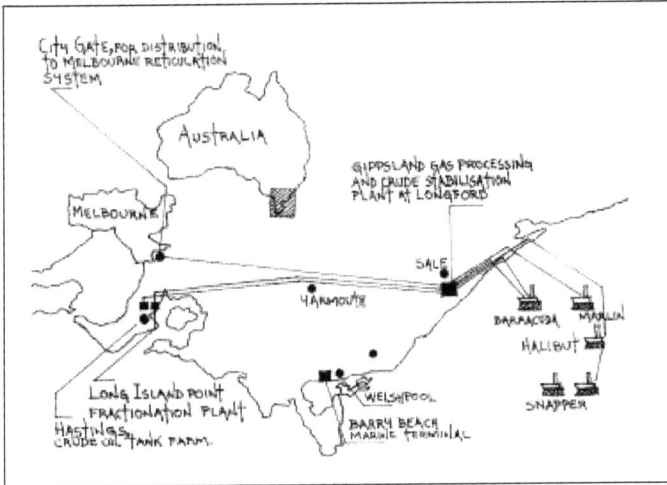

Esso Australia's Bass Straight developments
1969

were connected by pipeline to a gas processing and crude stabilization plant at Longford, near Sale, Victoria. The processed gas was pipelined to Melbourne, then a city of two and a half million. Esso had given a corporate guarantee to deliver natural gas by April 1969, and we made it. The oil and gas liquids were pipelined to a fractionation plant and export tank farm at Hastings on Long Island Point. At that time Australia consumed more or less 500,000 barrels of oil per day and produced more or less 60,000 barrels per day from the Moonie Field in New South Wales and Barrow Island of the West Coast. When we brought the Halibut platform on production in 1969, we had the production up to 180,000 barrels per day within a week, and Australia was 40% self-sufficient, almost overnight. I understand these fields, like Redwater, are pretty well empty today.

I can say that when we arrived in 1967, Australia was as the Aussies say, "rough as a cob," very unlike the country it is today. We left in 1971 by riding the Indian-Pacific train to Perth and flying to Indonesia, our next posting. I revisited Australia for a

Barry's Beach Yard, where Esso constructed platforms for Bass Strait
Victoria, Australia, 1968

month in 2001 and was so pleased with what I saw. Australia today is a clean, organized, well-serviced country with a confident,
efficient population.

Chapter 14

Indonesia

We left from Sydney, our last posting in Australia, in 1971. P.T. Stanvac, the Esso affiliate in Indonesia, had negotiated a new exploration block in southern Sumatra, called the Corridor Block. After several years of civil unrest, during which Suharto had put Sukarno out, it looked as though things were stabilizing. Leaders emerge in war time, for example Patton, Churchill, Montgomery, Ataturk, etc., and Sukarno was one of those. After 400 years under Dutch absolute domination, the Japanese had put the Dutch out during World War II. When the war ended the Dutch tried to come back in, assisted by the Brits who supported them from Singapore (not the Brits' proudest moment), and they were stopped by Sukarno, who marshalled the Indonesian forces and held them off. Not trained to rule, Sukarno made a lot of mistakes, most notably with corruption, and succumbed to a coup by Shuharto in 1969.

Esso had a long history in Indonesia, and P.T. Stanvac was a 50:50 company, Esso and Mobil Oil. Stanvac was staffed with Esso personnel. They had operated two oil fields in the jungles of Sumatra, Pendopo and Lirik, since the 1920s, excluding the World War II years when the Japanese operated those oil fields. The camps in the Sumatran jungle were typical American built oil camps of the kind I have seen through the years at Talhara, Peru, Abqaiq, Saudi Arabia and Las Monas, Colombia. P.T. Stanvac had operated a refinery at Palembang in the South of Sumatra, which had since been nationalized and rolled into Pertamina, one of the first state oil companies in the global trend towards nationalizing oil and gas operations as the price of oil shot up. Petro Canada was just another example of this trend.

The "contract of work", whereby an oil company does not hold title but works an oil field or block under contract to a state oil company was pioneered in Indonesia about this time. It was a little hard to accept by the majors, but is now commonly used.

Bejak taxis for hire
Block M, Djakarta, 1971

Any similarity between Djakarta today and in the early 1970s would be only coincidental. This was the most populous Muslim country on the planet. Housing was hard to find. There was no telephone service. The conductors in the electric distribution system were so undersized that at peak hours the voltage would drop and the current would go up and the high amperage would burn out air conditioners, etc. The roads were unpaved and plugged with traffic, since drivers took the children back and forth to school and ladies sent messages to friends with their drivers because there was no phone system. There was little for sale in the local market except fruit and vegetables, so the company arranged for us to import a $100 shipment of food each month from Singapore.

I spent most of my time in the oil fields in Sumatra. In due course, after drilling a number of dry holes with a Peter

Bawden drilling rig, Esso relinquished the Corridor Block. The block was later contracted by Bow Valley Industries who went on to discover oil there. There was a lot to be done, and the Indonesian employees were super helpful. I found the Indonesian people generally bright, attractive, happy and artistic, but superstitious; many believed that spirits lived in trees.

Chapter 15

The Beaufort Sea

In the spring of 1972 in Djakarta, I learned that the Canadian Government was advertising some amazing jobs in the Beaufort Sea for engineers with offshore experience, so I reported for work in Ottawa in September of that year.

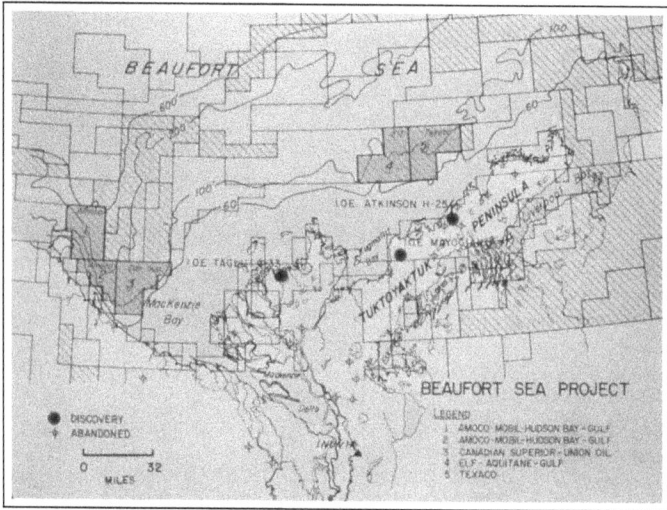

Leasing program in the Beaufort Sea
1975

The Northern Development Department of the Canadian Department of Indian and Northern Affairs (DINA), had done an amazing job of leasing up vast tracts of the Beaufort Sea, ice covered for probably eight months of the year. The hydro-carbon rich Mississippi Delta was occasionally mentioned as a model for

48

the Mackenzie River Delta. From time to time over the next two years I would ask myself, "Why are we doing this," whereupon I would tell myself, "If all these oil companies want to do this, let's go." Though my years in this fascinating business I have observed how faddish oil companies are; if one goes to SE Asia or the Beaufort Sea, they all go. If one goes into minerals they all go.

My first assignment was to organize a conference on exploration-drilling in the Beaufort Sea. We invited each of the companies that had taken leases and drilling companies to make presentations. We had senior executives from Global Marine, Sedco, Penrod, Kenting, Dome Petroleum, Hunt Oil, Panarctic, Gulf Oil, Imperial, Shell, and others. It was said that when Bunker Hunt got back to Dallas and someone asked him what he had learned in Ottawa he replied, "I learned that there is no way a fat boy from Dallas is going to drill in the Beaufort Sea."

Drilling at Moikka Fiord
Axel Heilberg Island, 1973

I participated in drilling inspection trips to the Arctic, to Inuvik and drilling operations in the Delta for Shell and Imperial as well as to Axel Heiberg and Ellesmere Islands, and once with a stop at Resolute on Cornwallis Island. I was twice invited to Halifax by Sedco for christenings of offshore drilling rigs, the Sedneth 704 under contract to Ranger Oil in 1973 and the Sedco 701 under contract to Mobil Oil in 1974. Sedco had enjoyed the ship-building subsidies contributed by the Canadian Government.

An important aspect of the conference, one we never discussed, was for us to learn what the oil companies knew and/or planned to do. In due course we received applications from Imperial to drill from man-made, so-called artificial islands, from Dome to drill using drill ships, from Panartic to drill from ice islands and finally, after I had left DINA, from Gulf to drill from a specifically designed ice resistant structure. I worked closely with the Department of Transport, which at that time had developed pioneering regulations for an Arctic Class of vessels. I did the assessments of these submissions, approved them technically and put them forward for official approval. The applications were well considered and complete; a major concern was to protect the pristine arctic environment, particularly from oil spills.

Chapter 16

USSR/Canada Technical Exchange

In 1972 and 73, I was appointed to the USSR-Canada Drilling Subcommittee of the joint USSR-Canada Oil and Gas Committee. At that time, Russia had joint committees, largely by the initiative of President Brezhnev, in a number of industries with a number of countries. The Chairman of our committee was Scov Murray from Imperial Oil. I served as the Secretary, and the other members were Archie Jones from Shell, Jim Davidson from S&T Drilling, Tony Vandenbrink from Kenting, Sandy Purdy from Gulf and Walt Zaruby from Westburne Drilling. Scov was a legend in the industry for his ability to get things done and his technical creativity.

Canadian-Russian Oil-Gas Technical Exchange Committee
Imperial Oil offices, Calgary, 1975

The Soviet Committee consisted of Y.A. Teretyev, Chief of the Drilling Department and Board Member of the Oil Ministry; I.S. Borodin, Drilling Expert in the Oil Ministry; V.I. Belav, Deputy Director of Drilling and Production in Tumen; and Dr. V.I. Ryhabchenko, Deputy Director, Drilling Research Institute in Krasnodar. The exchange started with a visit from the Soviet Committee in March of 1973. We toured a number of drilling sites in the Arctic, the Petroleum Training Institute at Edmonton and the Arctic Research Institute at Inuvik, and then held a series of meetings in Calgary.

Canadian and USSR delegates visit Arctic drill sites
March, 1973

On an inspection trip in the spring of 1973 to Inuvik we flew out to observe a seismic crew in operation on the ice. The crew was supported by a camp made up of a series of sled-mounted trailers pulled by Caterpillar tractors. Shortly before we arrived that day, one of the cooks had stepped out of the kitchen trailer and been grabbed by a polar bear, killed and dragged off. The crew managed to recover the body by chasing and surrounding the bear with Caterpillar tractors. At that time people were not permitted to have fire arms in the north; I believe that has changed.

Our mandate was to collaborate on a project of mutual interest, so much of our time was taken discussing what we could collaborate on. I can still recall Dr. Belav's comments, through an interpreter, "Our research department is studying the merits of horizontal drilling to increase the productivity and the useful life of oil fields." We looked at each other as if to say, "What is he talking about; we know how to directionally drill?" Some 20 years later horizontal drilling combined with fracking has become the major technical breakthrough of the century in North America. How it has been applied in Russia I do not know.

In October 1973 we toured the Soviet oilfields, Kuybyshev, Krasnodar and Tyumen in Siberia, followed by a weekend on the Black Sea at Sochi. What we called "Management by Objectives" the Russians called "Five Year Plans". The crew that drilled the most footage for the year in Siberia, spent Christmas in Cuba. I accidentally met Norval Jackson, Missouri School of Mines, at Krasnoda. We had worked together at EPRCo. Norval told me he was building a Security rock bit factory there; this was 1973. From that and when I saw the hordes of Caterpillar tractors in the oilfields, I concluded that the much touted American-Russian ideological Cold War must have made some exceptions for commercial interests.

Russia was a very different place then. We were issued food stamps to use during our stay, we saw *The Barber of Seville* performed at the Bolshoi and witnessed the real Russia of the time. We learned the elements of Russian toasting early on: you must tell a little story, preferably with a point, and then knock it back. At our first lunch at a rig we were keen, not interested in vodka, until the Tool Pusher made a toast observing that these Canadians eat and drink like ladies. That did it!

Chapter 17

Saudi Arabia

After two years in Ottawa I decided I related more to producing oil than regulating it, and so in September, 1974 I joined Aramco in Dhahran, Saudi Arabia. These were the boom years worldwide. Aramco pulled out all stops and in response to market demand production peaked at over 11 million barrels per day; I would suggest that might remain an all-time high for Aramco. It was fascinating, as here was the world's major oil producing company, owned by the four majors, Chevron, Texaco, Mobil and Esso, a great structured company, under serious pressure to prepare for the future.

I first worked in the Petroleum Engineering Department, went on to supervise one of the Petroleum Engineering Divisions, and was then transferred to the Production Department as Superintendent of one of the five Producing Divisions. Ali Naimi, now the Saudi Oil Minister and previously the Secretary General of OPEC, now known as H.E. Ali bin Ibrahim al Naimi, was head of the Producing Department at that time.

Aramco had no gas gathering system then, and all of the natural gas was flared. When production increased to 11 million barrels, more or less three billion cubic feet of gas was flared and burned per day. From the air you could see the flares from a great distance.

To that time Aramco had no water-treating facilities in the field either. These big wells, producing from bottom drive reef reservoirs, would go to a high salt content before producing water so we monitored the salt content; when the salt content at a well reached 100 pounds per thousand barrels we simply shut the well in.

David Benediktson, front left; Ali Naimi, Production Manager,
front center; Steve Benediktson, third from left
Awards night, Abqiaq Production Division, 1976

To that time Aramco did not test individual wells. In fact there were no well-test facilities in the field. We tested some wells using a portable turbine meter installed in a by-pass from which individual well-production was estimated. Oil was carefully measured onto the export tankers at Ras Tanura. Aramco at that time did not have a significant pressure-maintenance system in place. The north end of the giant Ghawar Field was dump-flooded from the Wasia aquifer, and we estimated the dump-flooding rate periodically with turbine meters run on a wire line.

All of that has been changed, most dramatically after the Saudi government nationalized the industry and Aramco became a contractor to Saudi Aramco, the state oil company. All natural gas is now gathered and processed and commercialized. A sea water treating plant has been commissioned to treat and inject ten million barrels per day of water for pressure maintenance. Water treating facilities have been added. Aramco has grown from 15,000 to 50,000 employees.

In 1977, I represented Aramco's Producing Department on

the Gas Gathering Project, which was designed in Fluor's engineering office's in Houston. On one of my return trips from Houston to Dhahran, at the last moment I decided to stop at Susan's school as it was their Father's Day weekend. The Saudi Ruler to that time had not allowed any high schools in the Kingdom for expatriate children, as was his prerogative, and when Susan left Saudi to attend high school she went to a school called Foxcroft at Middleburg, Virginia.

I flew to Dulles, rented a car, drove to Middleburg, visited Bloomingdale's at Tyson's Corner, their first branch out of Manhattan, with Susan, then turned to finding a place to stay. As I passed The Fox and Hound in Middleburg, the oldest inn in America, I decided to check with them and to my delight the clerk told me they had just received a cancellation. When the clerk showed me the room he commented, "The last Canadian to stay in this room was Margret Trudeau." When she left Trudeau, Margret embarked on a photographic career, and Rupert Murdock had brought her to Middleburg to introduce her to Elizabeth Taylor who lived on a farm nearby with her husband, Secretary of Defense Warner. The clerk said, "There was no hanky-panky," but most remarkably, I have slept in the same bed that Margret Trudeau slept in.

At one time I was responsible for testing the Shayba discovery well in the Rub Al Kwali, the famous Empty Quarter with the enormous sand dunes, which is now on production. I remember a Bedouin arriving in camp out of those sand dunes with his camel, a few goats, a couple of wives and a few children. He came forward to greet me and touched his heart with great dignity. This was a follower of the Prophet Mohammed, and he knew exactly who he was and where he was.

On a visit to Saudi Arabia in 2009, I was asked to make a presentation to the Amir of the Province of Mecca, Khaled Al-Faisal, in his Reception in Jeddah on behalf of the visiting ex-Aramcons. His father, King Faisal, a hard working man, who used to drive himself to work each day, was the Ruler of the Kingdom when we arrived in the Kingdom, until he was assassinated by one of his nephews.

Benediktson presenting a gift to the Amir of the Province of Mecca
Jeddah, 2009

Saudi was a great work experience and gave us the opportunity to take some very special trips. We did a game park tour
of Kenya and Tanzania in 1976, and a number times we flew to
Iran for long weekends, either Isfahan or Shiraz or Tehran.

Chapter 18

Abu Dhabi

In September 1977, I accepted the position of Vice President of Drilling and Production with Amerada Hess Corporation back in Calgary. We had been away from Alberta since more or less 1965, and it seemed that it was only a place to visit grandmother and the cousins. It was good to get caught up in the country and the industry. The work was challenging, and the people were excellent to work with; the main operations were at Olds, Ferrier and Sturgeon Lake.

In 1980 the company needed a General Manager for their operations in the United Arab Emirates, based in Abu Dhabi. Leon Hess learned that I had spent a number of years in the Middle East, and in due course I took over that operation. I have been "under water" so to speak a couple of times in my career, and that was one of them. In addition to the offshore production operation with facilities on Arzanah Island, storage in a captive tanker, the Tropical Lion, I inherited some 250 employees, a Sedco jack-up drilling operation, a major camp construction project with Brown and Root and sub-contractor Hyundai, the need for a pressure maintenance project and coordination with the Petroleum Ministry.

After the camp was completed we held an inauguration ceremony, hosting Crown Prince H.H. Sheik Khalifah bin Zayed Bin Sultan al Nabayan, now the ruler; Dr. Mana Saeed Al Otaiba, Energy Minister and then Chairman of OPEC; Hess executives – CEO Leon, President Phil Kramer, Directors Richards Sellers, Bob Hearin and Mac McCallum; as well as our partner representatives – Bill Harris and Dr. Fred Wellhauser from Bow Valley, Larry Miskew and Bob Stannich from Canadian Superior,

Leon Hess and Shaik Khalifa, Benediktson behind Sheik Khalifa
Abu Dhabi, 1981

L. Challmer and W. MacDonald from Marathon, H. Mitchell and Sheik Farid from Kerr McGee and Angus MacKenzie and his son Norman of Sunningdale Oil.

Having an island conveniently located for processing the off-shore production was a real plus: no helicopters required. We serviced the island with an Otter air-craft. The staff had a base-ball diamond, etc. In the early 1980s Abu Dhabi was a shadow of its present self. Staffing and housing was a problem. We needed a geologist and hired Nabilo Khouri from Calgary; we needed a Chief Engineer and hired Dr. Sami Razza from Aramco; we needed an Island Manager and hired John Rebold, at one time my boss in Aramco.

My times with Leon Hess through those years were a real pleasure; this included on one occasion signing up a new concession in Abu Dhabi with Dr. Armand Hammer of Occidental Petroleum accompanied by his then president Robert Abboud and Ali Al Fayed, Doddi Al Fayed's uncle. The split was 50/33.3/16.7%. Leon was a giant of the industry who made things happen.

The Arzanah field partners Operating Committee
Abu Dhabi, 1981

One morning in 1981 we discovered that all inbound flights had been diverted to Dubai. It turned out that Saddam Hussein had attacked Iran and that the Iraqi fighter planes were being re-fuelled in Abu Dhabi at night. The American Ambassador to the United Arab Emirates called and we discussed evacuation; I was managing the only operating American oil company in the UAE at the time. We concluded that this was probably a border skirmish that would last a few weeks. It lasted eight years with hundreds of thousands of deaths and millions of dollars of property damage. Saddam Hussein was a very bad man and needed to be dealt with. The Bush Administration had the justifiable opportunity to put Hussein out when he invaded Kuwait in 1990 but for some curious reason did not.

The American invasion of Iraq, March 19, 2003, was presented by the American media as an "American Sporting Event". The American media has a way of putting a spin on things. At first President Bush spoke of terrorism and the hunt for "weapons of mass destruction". America had to protect the "homeland"

The Hess production facilities in the United Arab Emirates
Arzanah Island

and it became a war with Iraq. Iraq had no weapons of mass destruction, and it was not a war with Iraq. It was an invasion of Iraq by the Americans. Iraq, a country of some 26 million people located in the Middle East, did not present a serious threat to the world or to the United States, a country of 319 million people with the most powerful military establishment in history. The media presented the invasion in detail discussing the advances of "our brave troops" against the Iraqis.

President Bush talked about liberating the Iraqis, but they did not want to be liberated with bombs and shelling to kill them, their friends and relatives. This was an atrocity inflicted on a poor Arab country by the Americans for a variety of reasons, most notably egos, the symbolic punishment of the guilty for September 11, 2001, American politics and commercial motives. Thousands of innocent people were killed, their homes and property destroyed, and billions of dollars of Iraqi property were destroyed by the American bombing and shelling. The Iraqis bravely defended their country against a foreign invader, as many of us would have done for our home lands, knowing that

61

the final outcome could only be death and defeat at the hands of a far superior enemy.

The world witnessed an atrocity on a scale that has seen no precedent when Bush invaded Iraq. Since the USSR imploded there had been no offset to America's power. The world witnessed America ignoring world opinion, ignoring the United Nations as an agency to provide a consensus of world opinion and, essentially unilaterally, invading a country that logic said was no threat to America and no equal to the American military might. The significance of this was far-reaching. Consider America's future action should the American establishment decide they need Canada's water or Mexico's oil; we have witnessed America in action.

George W. Bush should have been charged and tried for war crimes as a result of his part in the Iraq War. Hundreds of thousands of innocent Iraqis were killed, and hundreds of thousands of dollars' worth of Iraqi property, much of it historic and irreplaceable, was destroyed as a direct result of that attack. The attack was prompted largely by circumstantial evidence that was later found to be false. Bush not only destroyed Iraq, but he seriously damaged America's image around the world. Moreover, Bush was directly responsible for the death of thousands of Americans in that war and planted the incubator for ISIS which has been responsible for many thousands more.

In 1980 we took a memorable trip to India from Abu Dhabi; we visited Delhi and went on to Srinagar, capital of the province of Kashmir in the Himalayan mountains in the northwest corner of India. Very beautiful, we stayed in a bed and breakfast house boat, of which there were many on Dal Lake in the city. All manner of services and products were available from peddlers in sampans each day, from fresh bread in the mornings and flowers to tailors, barbers and masseuses. Unfortunately soon after that all tourism to Srinagar ended with the outbreak of armed hostilities between the Moslem majority and Hindu India, which continues.

Chapter 19

Argentina

In 1981, I returned to Calgary and, in partnership with the Al Fayed brothers, Mohammed, Ali and Saleh, started a company – Benson International Oil and Gas Services Ltd. The Al Fayeds wanted to establish a position in oil and gas; in addition to their interests in Dubia and the Ritz Hotel in Paris, they had recently acquired Harrods store in London, and Mohammed's son Dodi had produced the award winning movie, *Chariots of Fire*. Unfortunately, I was unable to bring forward an oil and gas investment of sufficient interest and our partnership was dissolved after one year.

Benson had various clients, including Dennison at Kavala, Greece and Deminex at Essen, Germany, where I placed my friend from Aramco days, Said Arrata. In 1983 Robert Jones called from Booz Allen & Hamilton in New York and asked if I would join them in an organizational study for a family-owned oil company in Argentina. I agreed and, after two trips to Argentina to meet the Bulgheronis and to view Bridas SAPIC's operations, the Bulgheronis invited me to take over the position of Director General of the company. The incumbent, Glenn Nelle, an elderly Texan, had retired.

This was one of the times in my career where I was "under water", because I knew no Spanish. In 1983, after the Falklands War but still under military rule, Argentina was a very different place than it is today. A very closed and reserved society, people gave you their business cards with only their names on them. Very few people spoke English. I have always worked hard, but the hardest I ever worked was in Argentina during those years. We were at the office by 7:00 a.m., rarely left before 8:00 p.m., and the Bulgheronis frequently called meetings on Saturday mornings. If we went out for dinner we never went before 9:00 pm. This dedicated work ethic has resulted in Carlos and Alejandro becoming billionaires, as reported in *Forbes Magazine*'s 2015 list.

Arturo Illia, then President of Argentina, had nationalized the oil and gas industry in 1963, and it must be said that Argentina generally paid companies book value when expropriating their assets. It had significant gold reserves at the end of World War II, and when Peron expropriated the railways from the British, a politically popular move, the country paid cash.

The state oil company, YPF, had recently assigned various fields to Argentine companies: Bridas, Pluspetrol, Perez Compan, CAPSA, Astra and CGG. Birdas had received the Piedra Clavada and El Cordon fields at Pico Truncada, near Comodoro Rivadavia and the Lindero Atravesado and Fernandez Oro fields at Neuquen. Bridas had also taken an exploration block, the Acambuco, in the Salta Province at Tartagal near the Bolivian border, an interest in a block in the Austral Basin, offshore Tierra del Fuego with Total and Deminex and had an interest in a production block with Occidental Petroleum at Tahlara, Peru. While I was with Bridas, we drilled three dry exploration wells on the Acambuco block in Salta Provimce, the most expensive onshore wells that I have ever been involved with. This was deep, difficult drilling through sloughing shale formations.

My years in Argentina were action packed, full of new experiences. I grew to love Argentina and Buenos Aires, the Paris of South America. In 1984, Argentina returned to democracy and elected Raul Alfonsin of the Radical Party as President. By 1985, the Government, in search of ways to attract investment capital, prepared a program for leasing oil and gas lands and were ready to present that to the international oil industry. When planning the presentations, I suggested to Rodolfo Otero, then President of YPF, that they should present in Canada. As a result, in September of 1984 we presented in Calgary and Ottawa. The delegation was headed by the Secretary of Energy, Dr. Conrado Storani, who coincidentally had been Secretary of

Energy in 1963 when Argentina nationalized the industry.

Argentina went on to pioneer the idea of Marginal Field Contracts, where the decline curve for a field is agreed upon. A contractor then agrees to an investment schedule for field improvements, and the incremental additional production is shared in parts between the contractor and the state oil company. Argentina is regrettably not a major "oil province". I attended Schlumberger's 50 year celebration in Argentina in 1988. This was the second country Schlumberger offered their services to, and I thought to myself, "They are still producing less than 500,000 barrels per day," now up to more or less 700,000.

Argentina suffered from hyper-inflation, and we gave everybody a cost of living raise of between 25 and 35% per month. Devaluations occurred regularly, once with a currency name change from Pesos to Australs. Nothing at all seemed to work until the Menem administration pegged the peso to the dollar. That worked until Argentine products became so expensive that exports dried up and unemployment climbed to over 20%. The administrative burden that inflation created for the industry and the government was immense.

As time permitted in Argentina I played polo; polo is a passion for most people that play it. I grew to know many people in Argentina's world of polo at the time, including the Blaquire family. As I recall, at that time there were only some 3,000 people with polo handicaps, worldwide, and Churchill had famously said that a polo handicap was a passport to the world.

One week end Maleyna Blaquier invited me out to their estancia Conception, one of the foremost classic Argentine estancias, where she lodged me in the guest house. Maleyna told me stories of the many notables who had visited and played polo at Conception, including Prince Phillip when he visited Argentina in the 1950's. Maleyna, who in her time was unquestionably the most beautiful lady in Buenos Aires, had four daughters at home at that time, equally as attractive. She told me that Phillip enjoyed himself so much that he called the Queen from there to explain he was going to stay a few more days at Conception.

Maleyna also told me that she had lodged Prince Phillip in that same guest house; think of it, I have slept in the same bed that Prince Philip slept in.

One of my most memorable flights ever was when I was returning from a partners meeting at Totals offices in Paris via Toronto, and I checked in behind a big fellow wearing a green cowboy hat: Eugene Whalen. We hit it off immediately, sat together and never stopped talking until we got to Toronto. Whalen had been Minister of Agriculture under Trudeau. When John Turner succeeded Trudeau, he dismissed Whalen, who had relocated to Rome as Canada's Representative to the World Health and Food Administration. When Mulroney then defeated Turner at the polls, Mulroney changed Representatives. After a couple of Scotches, Whalen laughed, "I've been fired by two Prime Ministers within a year." We exchanged Christmas cards until he passed away a few years ago.

Amongst the unique features of Argentina at the time was the telephone system. It took years to get telephone service in your home, and even then it was almost impossible to get an international connection. My secretary, Roberto Ingledew, came to the office one day chuckling and said, "My friend got his first telephone yesterday; he applied 20 years ago. I have never had to wait more than four years for a telephone."

Chapter 20

Making an Oil Company

I decided to return to Alberta and start an oil company. The Alberta Stock Exchange had just initiated the Junior Capital Pool program, and in early 1988 I floated Benson Petroleum Ltd. as a JCP company and was then in search of a "major transaction", as required under the program. We first acquired Juggernaut Resources and two packages of properties from Illyas Choudry at Saba Petroleum, and in due course we acquired producing properties at Westlock, Didsbury, Cessford, Holden, Shauvon and Cherhill in Alberta, Fireweed-Inga in British Colombia and exploration properties in the foothills.

The oil industry is a very capital intensive business, and a good part of our time and energy was involved in raising capital and banking. We soon learned where to go to look for capital – Toronto, Montreal, New York and London – and what the money men wanted to hear. We joined the industry associations, which are a great help in Canada. I was able to attract a fine Board of Directors, which was important notwithstanding my opinion that outside Directors, as required to protect shareholders of public companies, play a limited role in the corporate world.

I had the very good fortune to attract good people to work with me. Early in 1990, I acquired an interest in and took over an operation in Colombia, and Steve, my oldest son and an exploration geologist, agreed to join me. Industry has a lot of reservations about nepotism; personally I like family companies. In our search for investment capital, if we went together someone would inevitably say, "But you have the same names," as though that was not allowed. The major international merchant banks attest to the fact that there are distinct strengths in fam-

Steve Benediktson at the first well drilled by Benson Petroleum
Cherhill field, 1991

ily companies. A few years later it was my good fortune to have Yook Mah join us; an excellent team. Coincidentally all three of us had graduated from high school in Red Deer; the similarities ended there, which added to our team's strength.

I am like the old driller who said, "I've been at this so long I've seen nine inch hole declared the optimum hole size three times." We have seen dry holes drilled between two producers; "Mother Nature is a Bitch". Accordingly, Benson avoided drilling for the first years; we acquired producing properties, generally marginal production and enhanced them. The first well drilled by Benson was an excellent producer at Cherhill.

Benson Petroleum had a 14 year life. In early 2000, we were the targets of a so-called "hostile" take over. All things considered, we negotiated a sale and purchase price and turned over our properties. I finally admitted that it gets cold in Alberta and retired to Central Mexico.

The high points of my career in the oil business were making Benson Petroleum Ltd. and PetroSantander Inc. Business was almost always fascinating for me and doing a start-up and operating a public company was very special, particularly the interface with the investors.

Benson had more than its fair share of diverse investors and shareholders. For example Bobby Monroe, a graduate of MIT from the famous American Monroe family, managed Uncle Edgar's foundation. One of the first things Bobby did when he took over management of the foundation was to give Uncle Edgar's summer home, Rosecliff at Newport Beach where the Great Gadsby was filmed, to the state. Nevertheless, when Bobby married Kim he held the wedding there with probably one hundred of his closest friends, including Adriana and I.

Chapter 21

Colombia

In late 1989, the telephone rang early one Saturday morning; it was Illyas Choudry. He told me that if I would like to buy Occidental's interest in the Las Monas Block in Colombia, to be in Bakersfield, California on Monday to sign it up. Illyas had held the block under an option to purchase for upwards of a year; we had talked about it some months before, but I had pretty well put it out of my mind. I had some knowledge of the block from my years in South America. Occidental were at the point of moving on with it. I called the Directors that I could find on a Saturday morning, who said to the effect, "If you think that is a good thing to do go ahead." Fortunately our Lawyer/Director Rick Wilson agreed to drop everything and join me.

Illyas picked us up at the airport at Bakersfeild and took us to a Mexican restaurant for lunch (I like Mexican), and negotiated the deal as between us. We then went to Oxy's office and negotiated the terms and conditions; to his great credit Rick worked through the night to paper the deal, and we were able to leave the next day for Calgary with a signed agreement. I had just negotiated a $100,000 line of credit with Roy Geick at the Royal Bank and casually left Oxy with a $100,000 down payment. My due diligence consisted of reviewing the Degolyer and McNaughton reserves report; we paid in the order of 75 cents per barrel for proven producing reserves, notwithstanding side issues such as assuming an unfunded pension obligation, security concerns and country risk. In 1989 the investment community asked, "What is a little Calgary junior oil doing international and particularly in Colombia?"

The Las Monas field is located in the Province of Santander,

Las Monas facilities operated by Petrolera Santander, a Benson Petroleum
Ltd. subsidiary.

an hour's fight from Bogota to Bucaramanga from where we
would chopper out 15 minutes to the field. Security was important; Oxy supported two army training camps on the block, and
we continued the practice. Company executives had guards and
travelled in armour plated vehicles, since some years earlier the
Head of Texaco in Bogota was found murdered in the trunk of
his car. At that time Colombia was the most violent country in
the world, with more or less 80 violent deaths per day, and the
murderers were rarely arrested. We were elected Operator by
the partners, took over some 80 employees and an equal number
of contract workers, set up an office and went to work. Security
in Colombia is much improved today, but it's still a concern.

My youngest son, David Benediktson, worked for the company in Bogota for the best part of a year and was a tremendous help for me. David, who has a degree in Fine Arts, has
since made significant contributions managing Special Effects in
a number of movies, most recently in the award winning movie
Revenant.

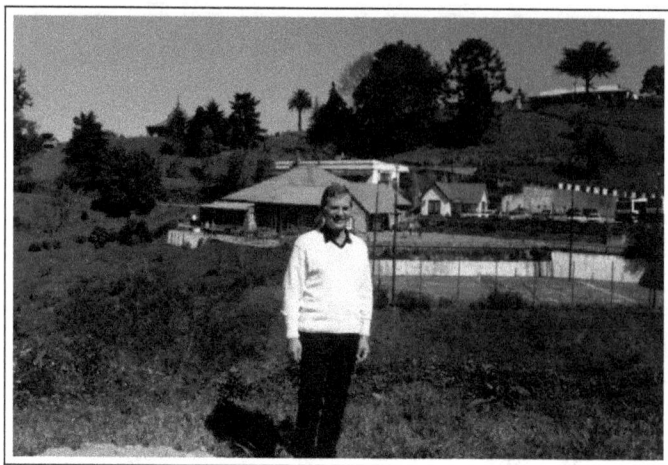

Las Monas camp near Sabana de Torres.
Santander, Colombia, 1991

Colombia is a beautiful country, nice people with an old, well established European culture. When I moved to Argentina in 1983, Colombia had the only democratically elected government in South America. Industry-wise, the work ethic is highly respected as is the sanctity of contracts. The anomaly is the guerrilla activity. When I arrived in 1990 and became aware of the problem, I thought, "This is ridiculous." I learned that the guerrilla establishment was originally communist inspired, funded in large part by the Soviet Union through Cuba. In due course, for reasons of politics and history, the Soviet funding ended and to survive the guerrillas turned to crime: kidnapping, robbing, and working as mercenaries for the drug industry. The guerrillas would stop cars and buses on the highways, rob the people, and generally burn or steal the cars and buses. It was not safe to travel by road from Bogota to Cartagena. During the years I was directly involved in our oil and gas operations in Santander Province, I never went into the nearby town of Sabena de Torres which was in the red zone. We maintained absolute confidentiality on executive field trips and travelled by helicopter from Bucaramanga to the heliport at the oil field where a few well-armed soldiers met us.

The following letter from the Colombian guerilla group, the ELN, was received by the company in January, 1999.

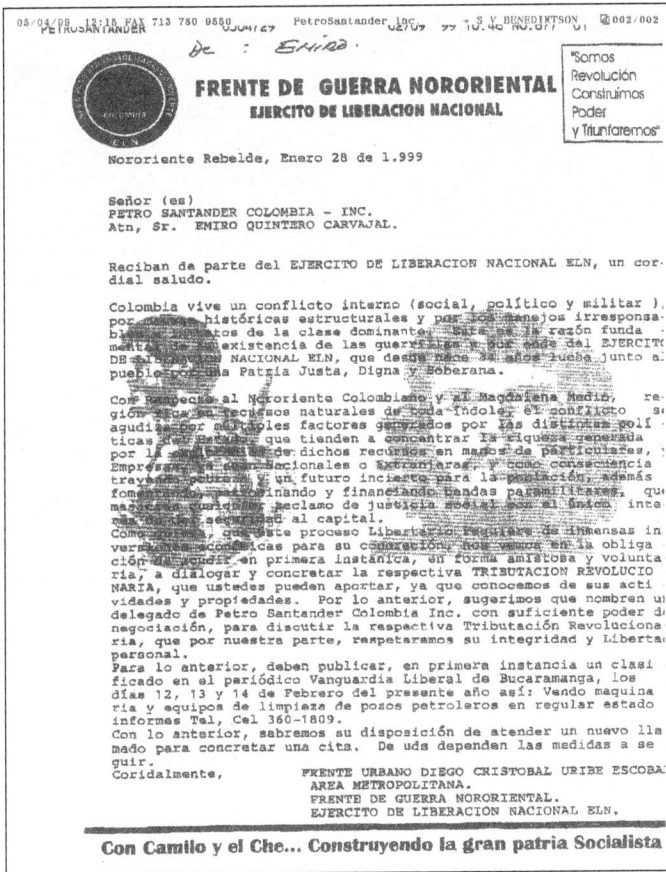

05/04/99 13:15 FAX 713 780 9550   PetroSantander Inc.   S V BENEDIKTSON   @002/002
PETROSANTANDER

De : Emiro

FRENTE DE GUERRA NORORIENTAL
EJERCITO DE LIBERACION NACIONAL

"Somos
Revolución
Construimos
Poder
y Triunfaremos"

Nororiente Rebelde, Enero 28 de 1.999

Señor (es)
PETRO SANTANDER COLOMBIA - INC.
Atn, Sr. EMIRO QUINTERO CARVAJAL.

Reciban de parte del EJERCITO DE LIBERACION NACIONAL ELN, un cordial saludo.

Colombia vive un conflicto interno (social, político y militar), por [...] históricas estructurales y por [...] manejos irresponsables [...] tos de la clase dominante, [...] la razón funda-menta [...] existencia de las guerri[...] del EJERCITO DE [...] NACIONAL ELN, que desea [...] junto a pueblo [...] la Patria Justa, Digna y Soberana.

Con respecto al Nororiente Colombiano y el Magdalena Medio, re-gión [...] recursos naturales de [...] índole, el conflicto se agudiza [...] múltiples factores generados por las distintas polí-ticas [...] Estado que tienden a concentrar la riqueza generada por [...] de dichos recursos en manos de particulares, Empresas [...] Nacionales o Extranjeras, y como consecuencia tray[...] pobre[...] y un futuro incierto para la población, además fom[...] financiando bandas para[...], que ma[...] reclamo de justicia social [...] al capital.

Com[...] este proceso Libertario requiere de inmensas in-ver[...] micas para su concreción, nos vemos en la obliga-ción [...] en primera instancia, en forma amistosa y volunta-ria, a dialogar y concretar la respectiva TRIBUTACION REVOLUCIO-NARIA, que ustedes pueden aportar, ya que conocemos de sus acti-vidades y propiedades. Por lo anterior, sugerimos que nombren un delegado de Petro Santander Colombia Inc. con suficiente poder de negociación, para discutir la respectiva Tributación Revolucionaria, que por nuestra parte, respetaremos su integridad y Libertad personal.

Para lo anterior, deben publicar, en primera instancia un clasi-ficado en el periódico Vanguardia Liberal de Bucaramanga, los días 12, 13 y 14 de Febrero del presente año asi: Vendo maquina-ria y equipos de limpieza de pozos petroleros en regular estado informes Tel, Cel 360-1809.

Con lo anterior, sabremos su disposición de atender un nuevo lla-mado para concretar una cita. De uds dependen las medidas a se-guir.

Coridalmente,

FRENTE URBANO DIEGO CRISTOBAL URIBE ESCOBA[...]
AREA METROPOLITANA.
FRENTE DE GUERRA NORORIENTAL.
EJERCITO DE LIBERACION NACIONAL ELN.

Con Camilo y el Che... Construyendo la gran patria Socialista

Letter from ELN

It is essentially a shake down letter, asking the company to make a "revolutionary contribution" in return for the ELN respecting our "personal integrity and freedom". We did not, of course, make any such contribution.[1]

Exxon operated the oil field adjacent to us. One day their head of security arrived at the local airstrip serving the two fields at the same time as our head of security arrived. A few moments later a squad of hooded, armed guerrillas appeared and took over. They marched the two security chiefs down the road a short way and shot and killed the Exxon man. Fortuitously our man was able to convince them, as they held a gun to his head, that he no longer worked in security, and they let him go.

In 2009, my wife Adriana and I visited her mother in Bogota. The common wisdom was that President Uribe was doing a good job of dealing with the guerrillas: one could now travel by car from Bogota to Cartagena safely, the taxis were generally safe to take, etc. As we relaxed after dinner we heard a muffled thud. When we got up in the morning we discovered that the guerrillas had set off a bomb in front of Blockbuster a few blocks away, killing two people, destroying the store and blowing the windows out of the high rise building across the street, but "things were much better".

My position throughout, which I have always freely expressed and still express, is that the President of Colombia should send the army in and tell the guerrillas to surrender or suffer the consequences. If this were Canada, or Sweden, or Germany or whatever country, that is what would happen. That would go a long ways towards solving the problems of lawlessness, murders, and kidnappings. Countries have armies and national guards to prevent such lawlessness. Why the Colombian government did not fix this problem I did not know, and why they would

---

[1]The footnote on the bottom of their stationary is interesting, "Con Camillo y el Che. . . Construyendo las gran patria Socialista." Camillo Torres was my mother in law's first cousin. He was a Catholic priest who had studied Political Science in Rome. When he returned to Colombia he started a socialist movement to help the Colombian poor. Camillo was shot and killed in a shoot out with the military; a General Tover wrote a book about him. Camillo's mother, Isabel Restrepo Gaviria, Elvira's Aunt, married Camillo's father, Calixto Torres Umanda in Hamburg, Germany in 1924. Isabel went on to become one of Castro's inner circle. She lived her later life in Cuba and died there in 1973.

negotiate with bands of criminals I could not understand until the television series *Narcos* was released; they buy everyone. Certainly it is well-known that corruption is a way of life in many parts of the world, particularly Latin America, and certainly we know that the drug business is big business in Colombia. Nevertheless, the Colombian government needs to fix this.

Chapter 22

International Deals

I pursued a contract in Libya in 1982, when Gaddafi was nationalizing the industry and the Libyan national oil companies
needed services. I chanced to stay at the Babel Bihar hotel in
Tripoli just as they were hosting a convention called "The General Congress of the World Centre for the Resistance of Imperialism, Zionism, Racism and Reaction." The delegates included
an incredible collection of dissidents from many countries and
there were stacks of hate information in the lobby. Gaddafi had
written, "The resistance of imperialism will be managed by all
oppressed peoples who will hold the mast on this sanctuary as a
sign of the beginning of collaboration of these peoples struggle
under the vests of this sanctuary."

In 1996, a London based Italian geophysicist came through
Calgary presenting a deal in Cuba that I liked a lot. A Swedish
entrepreneur and businessman, with no oil or gas experience, he
had discovered the deal in the Cuban Petroleum Ministry and
signed it up. When Castro took over and expropriated everything American, ARCO had held three petroleum leases contained in the offshore area by drawing a straight line from the
hook at the south east corner of Cuba to the centre of the island.

ARCO had ran a seismic program over the area just before
being nationalized, so when the Swede took title he received cans
of unprocessed seismic. He hired the Italian to have the seismic
processed, and to everybody's delight they found the blocks contained some 20 structures, including four elephants (petroleum
reserves of one billion barrels or more). Canada Northwest Lands
(Sherritt) took the blocks and the CEO, Fred Wellhauser, agreed
to let us have a ten percent working interest. We drilled one of

76

Benediktson and Peter Loughheed at an Arab / Canadian Conference
Calgary, Alberta, 1995

the prospects only to find it full of water; Mother Nature again.

Before I turned the operation of Las Monas in Colombia over to Chris Whyte in 1996, I introduced him to a deal, La Liebre, an outpost well that the owner had decided to sell. The closest oil field was Las Monas. Chris, a superb businessman and excellent negotiator, negotiated a deal for the well. It took over one year for the vendor to deliver good title during which time the net revenues accrued to the purchaser and the price of oil went up. When Chris picked up the clean title he received a cheque, net of the purchase price. The well is still producing.

In 1999 my friend Phil Paris had sourced a deal in Senegal, West Africa, which we went to look at. Phil, a seasoned oil and gas explorationist, Princeton 1947, had learned that the government held title to an outpost discovery well, not a major discovery, actually on the road to Timbuktu. We went to the field to look things over; a pipeline connection was the major hurdle. The Ministry official said the pipeline will have to run in that direction. I said, "What about that village that direction?" He replied, "They will move."

Part 3

Family

Chapter 23

The Legacy of Stephan G. Stephansson

The legacy of Stephan G. Stephansson is truly remarkable. He died in 1927, but when I consider the things that I have been involved with just this summer, 2010, it makes me stop and think about the whole thing: his *Biography*, an opera based on his *Pacifist Poetry*, an anthology of his work that is being published, a documentary film on him that was released with English subtitles in America, extracts of my Mother's book that have been published in the newspaper Loberg-Heimskringla, the Benediktson Fellowship for Icelandic Artists at the Banff Centre, registering Stephansson in the *Dictionary of Mid-Western Literature, Volume Two*, and some talk of a family saga.

George Rossato, my retired New York publisher friend, has familiarized himself with Stephansson and says that Stephansson was in the mold of Mahatma Gandhi and Martin Luther King. George has asked me if anyone in the family has surfaced that will pick up the ball on this whole thing when I am gone, and my reply was, "Not yet, but I am sure that one of them will."

As I reflect on what George says, I think back on what I know of the principle supporters of Stephansson's literary endeavours, starting around the turn of the century. First and foremost there was a Winnipeg Unitarian Minister named Rögnvaldur Pétursson and then an Icelander, Guðmundur Finnbogason, who was Iceland's National Librarian and Archivist at that time. In 1915 Finnbogason found himself in Winnipeg and was determined to see Stephansson on his visit to the New World. He took the train to Innisfail, Alberta, found someone to drive him out to the Stephansson farm at Markerville and spent a few days with the Poet.

Family

In the Markerville District, the leading activist supporter at that time was a farmer, Ofiegur Sigurdsson. I always remember him as dressed in a suit and tie and wearing a Homburg hat. He was a small but very upstanding, determined man. The monument at Stephansson's grave site is a testimonial to Ofeigur's determination to pay tribute to his friend Stephansson. It was totally privately funded in the depths of the Great Depression; donations were received from friends and family in Canada, the United States and Iceland.

In 1950 the Historic Sites and Monuments Board erected a cenotaph to Stephansson in the park at Markerville. In 1975 his old home near Markerville was opened as an Alberta Heritage Site, Stephansson House. In 1953 a monument was erected, funded by the Farmers Union of Iceland, close to his birth place in Northern Iceland. More recently, in 2003, a monument to Stephansson was unveiled on his original homestead near Mountain, North Dakota.

Through the years various individuals, mainly literary and academic figures, have studied and written about Stephansson and his work. Watson Kirkconnell, President of Acadia University, called him "Canada's Leading Poet" in an article about him in the *University of Toronto Quarterly* for 1936, and Stanton Cawley, professor at Harvard University, refers to him in *Scandinavian Studies and Notes* for 1938 as the greatest poet of the Western World, "greater than Poe, Whitman, or even Emerson."

Finnbogi Guðmundsson, the son of Guðmundur Finnbogason, was a life time supporter of Stephansson's. I first met Finnbogi when he came to Markerville enroute to Winnipeg to set up the Chair of Icelandic Studies at the University of Manitoba in 1952. We remained good friends and last visited him in Reykjavík in the summer of 2010. I can recall Finnbogi over 30 years ago telling me, "Stephan you must carry this on." At that time I was almost entirely focused on my work so I did not do a lot, but his comment remained with me and as time went on I have certainly responded to the challenge. Finnbogi returned to Iceland and took up the position his father had held many years before. The beautiful Reykjavík National Library stands

Unveiling of the Stephan G. Stephansson Cenotaph
Arnarstapi, Iceland – July 19, 1953

as a testimonial to Finnbogi.

The fascinating thing is that to this day new individual supporters and students of Stephansson's work continue to surface,
100 years after the fact. Most notably, the Icelandic Scholar,
Viðar Hreinsson, who dedicated more or less six years of his life
to researching and writing a biography of Stephansson. Over the
past year I have collaborated with Viðar on getting the biography translated and published in English; *Wakeful Nights Stephan
G. Stephansson: Icelandic-Canadian Poet* was published in 2013
and went on to win a Silver Medal for Non-fiction from the In-
dependent Publishers Association.

Sometime in 1998 the telephone rang in my office and a lady
who I never met told me that she worked for a film making
company, Great Northern Productions, a Division of Atlantic

Stephan G. Stephansson Monument.
Mountain, North Dakota

Alliance. She said they made a lot of films for television and were just embarking on a ten part series for the History Channel called *Journey Home* and that one part of the series was going to be on grandfather Stephansson. She asked me to work on the film with them, and of course I agreed.

During those years, I also had a call from a man who said he was with a film crew from Iceland en route to Markerville to make a film on Stephansson. They assembled a fine cast at Markerville, including Ron Stephansson, my Cousin Cecil's son, and made a documentary film. This summer they called back and said they were only now getting around to having the film fitted with English subtitles and released in America and asked me for financial support, which I provided.

When I was packing up my Mother's library to donate to the University of Manitoba, I found a manuscript that she had written. I recruited a talented young lady, Moorea Gray, to edit it and had the book published. Since then Moorea has visited Iceland, attended an Icelandic Conference in Winnipeg and prepared an Anthology of Stephansson's poems, complimented with photos of Iceland and Alberta. I have assisted with this project in some small ways.

The Benediktson Fellowship for Icelandic Artists at the Banff Centre continues to produce contacts with a succession of Visual Artists, Writers, and Composers, all with a connection to Stephansson. This connection will continue to provide pleasant opportunities for the individuals involved, The Banff Centre and the descendants of the Stephansson family, now and in the future.

A very especial discovery this summer, and one that serves to emphasise how the legacy lives on, was when I learned some time ago that the Head the Head of the Department of Music at the University of Calgary, Bill Jordan, had composed an opera based on the *Pacifist Poetry* of Stephan G. Stephansson. The opera is entitled *Vopnahle* (*Battle Pause*), after Stephansson's "flag ship" 24 page poem of the same name. The legacy lives on.

Bill, who was born and raised in Athens, Georgia earned his PhD in Music at University in Florida and then went to work at the University of Calgary. Bill discovered Stephansson soon after arriving in Alberta over 30 years ago and since then has read most of Stephansson's work that has been translated to English and has visited Markerville.

The pacifist part of Stephansson's character was central to his philosophy of life, although he addressed a considerable number of other issues ranging from women's rights, work, church doctrine, world government, free trade, etc. It took a great deal of courage as an immigrant in a British colony to write the type of pacifist work that he wrote:

> "In Europe's reeking slaughter-pen
> They mince the flesh of murdered men,
> While swinish merchants, snout in trough,
> Drink all the bloody profits off!"

There was talk of having him tried for treason. The legacy lives on, and it will be continued, though I am not sure how or by whom. Possibly a movie will be made about the life and times of Stephan G. Stephansson.

Vigdís Finnbogadóttir, President of Iceland from 1980 to 1996, the first lady President of any nation, world wide. worked with UNESCO for many years to establish an international language and culture centre. As the world becomes more united and standardized, we are in danger of losing many of the worlds diverse languages. As a result, the UNESCO Vigdis Institute of Foreign Languages, which is planned to open in 2017, has been constructed at the University of Iceland. In conjunction with that, it is planned to establish a chair at the University of Iceland entitled the Stephan G. Stephansson Professor in Migrant Literature. I supported that initiative and the related Endowment Fund.

Chapter 24

Speech by Stephan G. Stephansson

Stephan G. Stephansson's Speech on arrival in Reykjavík, June 17, 1917. Translator unknown.

The following speech was made at a banquet in Stephansson's honor at the City Theater Iðnaðarmannafélegshusid,[1] and Guðmundur Finnbogason delivered the main speech that night. The menu was salmon and stirred butter, veal with vegetables, biscuits, cheese, skyr with cream and coffee.

Honorable Ladies and Gentlemen:

I am not asking to be heard here at this eloquent gathering because of any illusions about my oratorical abilities. I do not often make speeches and if I do they are bad. The western plains and forests where I have lived for almost half a century, are the homes of silence: different from your country with the hum of the sea in every fjord, the purling of a stream in every vale and the murmur of a brook on every slope. I am talking here now because I felt that a humble speech would be less of an evil than accepting in complete silence everything you have so kindly done for me now and before.

I have a sense of being in the same position as the adventurers of old, who were destined to travel some untrodden paths but could not go until one day they found by their bedside some provisions and a new pair of shoes supplied by a friendly being

---

[1] Icelanders have a propensity for long, descriptive place names.

they hardly knew existed. This is why I am standing here, in order to express my sincere gratitude to all of you who are here now, and to convey in some way my thanks to all of those who gave their support when I was invited to Iceland. My sincere thanks for the invitation and this welcome.

To be sure, I would have been the last person I myself would have selected for this journey of honor, and people in America are not likely to have selected me either. To tell the truth, I hardly know how to explain my good fortune with you and with them.

It is true, however, that many people in America were so willing to grant me this pleasure, and your undertaking to invite a westerner to Iceland was so well received generally, whatever people's ideas of who would be the best choice, that I have no doubts everybody will be able to recognize the warmth shown towards us and feel kindly disposed towards you.

We all know well that I am not here on the account of my oratorical skills or the elegance of my good looks in a party of handsome men, and even though you are aware that I have forgotten many good habits in the remote west, I know that you will allow me to finish by reciting a little poem. As a matter of fact I can thank my dabbling in poetry that I am here now, and I was thinking of that when I sighted land and called it "From on Board Ship". It is like that:

From out of the sea, above the swelling deep
where lost and drowned worlds be buried,
I see mountain peaks emerge.
They are the white material hand of Iceland!
Over the blue ocean desert the Fatherland
rising in the sun, clad in the mantle of the dawn
welcomes you with open arms and spreads its light.
Behind me is yesterday's sun just above the horizon.
I came out on the rough sea without any favourable wind.
The return would not be so urgent
if my driving force had not been
like a youthful poem in the mouth of the east wind.

Restless as a Viking

How I long to thank those responsible
for my voyage and shake their hands.
when the shores of my cousins
beckon across the dark waves.
It is a blessing to be able, Lightly loaded,
to lower the sails in the harbors of relief.
What are hopes of return, poverty, or riches
after a long night of yearning?
A grown up child, with two empty hands,
I turn to you, ground of the dreams of my youth.
Sometimes it was fool's gold we found
on the other side of that wide strait.
I came to do no great deeds,
my native land. But I shall find in you
the alliterating rhythms of your waterfalls,
the silence of the mountains and the gold meant for me.
Because I choose to slumber in your lap,
peaceful and serene, and be rocked mildly and calmly
in the arms of sunshine and the embrace of your showers,
and wake over pleasure-dreams in the summer night.
I have come home to join your sons,
mother, to share the touch
of the deepest bonds that link me
with life and the wide world.
It would be no less joyful to come here
without any welcome prepared.
Come, blessed and beloved people
of my poems – just as you are.

On October 3, 2003, 150 years after Stephansson's birth, a book launch was held at the University of Iceland in Reykjavík for the second volume of the award winning biography of

Stephansson, *ANdvökuskáld* or *The Poet of Wakeful Nights*, by Icelandic Scholar, Viðar Hreinsson. Myself, Stephan V. Benediktson, grandson of Stephansson, delivered the keynote address at the book launch. That evening a banquet was held in the Iðnaðarmannafélegshusid, and Finnbogi Guðmundsson, son of Guðmundur, delivered the main speech. The menu was salmon and stirred butter, veal with vegetables, biscuits, cheese, skyr with cream and coffee.

Chapter 25

Siggi

Sigurdur (Siggi) Vilberg Benediktson, my father, was born at
Riverton, Manitoba on May 13, 1901 and died at Innisfail, Alberta on November 14, 1942. His parents were Benedikt Guðmundsson and Ingibjörg Guðmundsdóttir who immigrated to
Manitoba from the North of Iceland in 1900. His two older
sisters were born in Iceland. Two younger brothers, Karl and
Leo, and a sister were born in Manitoba. Two of the girls died
in a scarlet fever epidemic that swept through the settlement
in 1905, and his mother passed away in 1908. There is a good
write up on the family, with photos, included in a book called
The History of Arborg and District, 1889-1987.

After his mother died, Siggi was sent for and adopted by his
Great Uncle Sigurdur (Sam) Benediktson and his wife Vilborg of
Markerville, Alberta in 1911; Siggi was his namesake. He became
their son, took their name and assumed the responsibilities of the
farm. One social practice of Icelanders is how they take care of
their young; children are moved around in families as necessary
and appropriate. Sam and Vilborg lost their only child, Emil
Benedikt, in Iceland. When their fishing boat was wrecked and
sank, luckily with no loss of lives, they moved to the New World.
They settled at Markerville, Alberta, in 1902 and homesteaded
the NE/4-36-2-W5, one mile south of Heckla School, west of
Innisfail.

The Benediktsons had adopted a homeless young orphan in
Iceland, named Skuli. Unfortunately Skuli struggled with ill
health until he passed away at 18 years of age. A grave stone in
the Tindastoll Cemetery near Markerville memorializes the lives
of Skuli, Sam (1924) and Vilborg (1928). They were hard work-

ing pioneers; Sam enjoyed good literature and chess; Vilborg loved and always had many plants, made wreaths for funerals and did a lot of charity work. For a number of years Vilborg was President of the Icelandic Ladies Aid Club, Vonin. Their door was always open to hospitality and a homeless neighbor girl, Margret Bjornson, lived with them for several years, as did Olafia (Olive), Siggis surviving sister. Siggi married Rosa Stephansson, my mother, in 1928.

Sam and Vilborg built a new home on the farm in 1927, significantly up scale for the times. The house is illustrated on the cover of Rosa's book, *Looking Back Over My Shoulder*. This cost and the general economic difficulties of the "Dirty 30s" burdened Siggi with some debt. The Government organized a Debt Adjustment Board that enabled farmers to write off much of their debt at the time, but Siggi did not accept this largess; to him it seemed like accepting charity.

Siggi was well liked by all, a member of the Hecla School Board, and a Charter Member of the Friendship Lodge of the Knights of Pythias. Fond of sports, he was a good ball player, an avid reader, a skilled chess player, and he loved fishing. Entrepreneurial, Siggi and his two brothers commercially fished northern lakes in Alberta for several winters in the 1920s. Their fish was flown to New York and served fresh, unfrozen – a first.

A very hard worker, Siggi carried on with farming and trucking operations. At different times he hauled livestock, gravel and crude oil from Turner Valley to Edmonton; this was in the 1930s. He was a cattle buyer; bought cattle from farms and ranches in the area for the Adams, Wood and Weiller Company of Calgary, for which he received $1 per head. He could estimate the weight of a cow within a few pounds and do math, add, subtract, multiply and divide in his head, like today's computers.

Markerville was settled by a group of Icelandic settlers in 1988 and another group in 1989. A number of American families settled in the district; eleven families came from Nebraska around 1910, and in the 30s a number of other families came, escapees of the infamous Oklahoma Dust Bowl days. They added much to this frontier settlement, and many of their descendants remain in the district to this day. The Nelson brothers, Americans, were unquestionably the wealthiest farmers in the district; it was said they had arrived from the Klondike Gold Rush. Nels was married and John was a bachelor. Bill Fountain arrived from Oklahoma and married a Thomson, an Icelandic lady, and they had three boys and a girl. Sadly, as the boys reached their teens they lost their ability to walk and were confined to wheel chairs. They each passed away in their early twenties. The boys loved to play checkers with Siggi, who would play two of them at the same time.

I was only seven years old, but I can still remember when the Nelson brothers came to Dad to buy the farm for Bill Fountain, and in due course he agreed to sell out to them. He went on and bought what we called the Foozie-land across the road. This was a quarter of land, more or less a 60 acre field with about 100 heavily timbered acres below a bank on a flat leading to the Red Deer River, that Dad had rented from Foozie for years. Foozie was an elderly bachelor Icelander in the district who had unfortunately gone blind. I can remember he used to come and stay with us for a period of time each year. He used to chew tobacco, and it was not unusual to find one of his chews behind the curtains of a window, just too good to throw out. Curiously we had a second elderly Icelander who went blind, glaucoma I suppose, who would also come and stay with us for a period of time each year, Brandur Brandson.

Siggi constructed a road down the bank and a bunk house for us to live in on the Foozie-land, and that winter he and my Uncle Jake logged some of the timber off the 100 acres. Again, I can remember the Nelson brothers coming to offer to buy the Foozie-land from Dad, and eventually he agreed to sell it to them – hard decisions. Dad then purchased a bare quarter of land in the Tindastoll District some five miles east of Markerville. It had one grain bin on it that we used as a shelter that summer while Dad and my cousin Steve, a good carpenter, framed a small house on the hill looking west. Dad said it would become a chicken coop when he built Mother's dream home looking west.

They framed it, boarded it with shiplap boards then sid-

Siggi

ing, doors and windows and shingled it, and that was as far as
they got, no insulation or inside wall covering. We had a cook
stove and an air tight heater, a water well with a hand pump
for water and an outhouse for a toilet, no electricity or telephone and no shelter from the north west wind, not one tree.
The house remained essentially the same until Mother, Conrad
and Ted moved to Red Deer in 1953, except the inside walls
received wall board, without insulation, the airtight heater was

replaced with a Booker coal burning heater and a telephone was installed. Notwithstanding the better heater, both Mother and Ted suffered pneumonia twice through the next ten years.

On November 13, 1942, Dad took us to an auction sale in the Hecla District in his old farm truck; the farmer, Virgil Delong, had died at an early age. Dad complained of chest pains that day and curiously many years later when I attended the 100 anniversary party of the Hecla School, a neighbor Virgil Flake commented that Siggi was sick at Virgil Delong's auction sale. Both Virgils were from our American immigrant families. I have always thought that the name Virgil must have been popular in America around the turn of the century. Dad took some aspirins, and I remembered throughout those years that Dad often took aspirins.

That night Dad was in considerable pain, and Mother sent Iris to the neighbors to call Doctor Wagner to come out. He got lost and arrived late very irritated. I remember Mother, who was very concerned, asking him, "Doctor, what about his heart," and the Doctor telling her, "If Siggi dies of a heart attack he'll live to be a hundred." He left a bottle of Milk of Magnesia for Dad.

The next morning Dad got up, still in pain, and drove himself to the neighbors on the farm south of us, the Stokells, to ask someone to drive him into the hospital in Innisfail. We all kissed him goodbye; Iris was 13, I was 9, Conrad was 5 and Ted was 5 months old. Sometime later we looked up to see Mary Stokell, exhausted from running the mile to our house, saying "Siggi." Mother grabbed her coat and left on foot. That evening it was snowing heavily; mother arrived as she had left, on foot, with tears in her eyes. She cried a lot that first year, without the love of her life. Siggi had walked out of the Stokell's house and said, "Oh, Mrs Stokell," collapsed and died.

Mother did a remarkable job of survival, with almost nothing. There was no money, no income, some debt, no fuel for heat. We survived with a few cows, chickens and pigs and a garden. Iris and I fed the cattle and pigs before going to school, two miles away, far enough when it is 20 or 30 below zero. We walked or

Siggi and Rosa

rode a horse.

It never fails to amaze me when I think about it, but in the early 40s the Social Credit government of the day set up social payments, a monthly stipend per child under 16 and a pension for widows. When mother Rosa received the first Widow's Allowance check, $32, she sent it back; no thank you very much. She felt it would be accepting charity.

Mother sold Dad's old truck, and we did not have a car until 1945 when Uncle Jake sold his car to Mother, a 1935 Ford coupe; I recently found the receipt, $200. Mother had a lot of good qualities and strengths, but she was not very mechanically inclined. As a result, I was able to drive better than her, or I thought I could drive better than her, so I generally drove. I was 12 years old; fortunately road checks for driver's licenses were not that common in those days.

We survived: Iris married a neighbouring farm boy; I went to work on the rigs and a career in oil; Conrad apprenticed and became a licensed sheet metal worker, amongst other things; and Ted apprenticed and became a license plumber and pipefitter.

I must add somethings that come to mind as I wrote this, if nothing else but to help explain why I may be a little different, a survivor as they say. My first job was working for Einar Stephansson on his haying crew when I was 12; my pay was $2/day. A distant relative and good friend of my father's, Einar was the biggest farmer in the district. A graduate of Olds College, he had accumulated an amazing spread of land, cattle and pigs. The Hutterites later bought him out, and his farm became the Pine Hill Hutterite Colony. I drove a team of horses on a hay rake or sometimes pulled the stacker up, all different haying equipment in those days. I slept in the bunk house with the hired men. We got up soon after 7:00 a.m. to feed the horses before breakfast and then went to work.

One day when I was on the team pulling the stacker up, something broke. The cable came looping back, and as I turn my head it hit me in the mouth, cut my lip and broke the bottom off one of my front teeth. That evening, after work, Einar drove me into Innisfail, and Dr. Wagner put a couple of stitches in my lip – no freezing. Einar held my arms while Wagner did the stitching. Five or six years later the tooth turned black, and I had to have it taken out and a false tooth put in.

The Red Deer Composite High School was started in the old army camp in 1947, a boarding school, and mother sent me there. I had graduated from Grade 9 at Tindastoll School that spring when I was still 13 years old. That fall in threshing time I went home one weekend and went to work on Eric Thorsen's threshing crew the next day – $10/day plus $2/day for your team and wagon, big money. I was gone for two weeks, and when I went back to school with over $140 earned, Mother came with me; she seemed to sense I might need some support. I was taken to the office of Principal Whitney, a volatile returned vet. There I got one of the most serious lectures of my life; mother turned beet red. I can still remember him saying, "Boy you have to decide; are you going to school or going to work." Some ten years later when I went back to finish high school I had to take a math course from Mr. Whitney and several times had to listen to him give lectures about "young know-it-alls who go off to work without finishing their education".

During my high school dropout years I did whatever I could find to do. Driving a truck paid better than a lot of other things, but for that you needed to be 18 to get a chauffer's license, so when I turned 17, I applied. When they asked me how old I was, I said 18, and they gave me the license. That fall, 1950, after harvesting, Jesse Bourne's brother-in-law, Leo Proctor, came by on his way home to Whitehorse and told me if I was in Whitehorse he would give me a job driving a truck at his sawmill. He supplied timber to the mines at Keno Hill, north of Whitehorse, so after Christmas I hitch hiked the Alaska Highway to Whitehorse and worked there in 1951. That spring I flew home, my first commercial fight, to Edmonton with seed money in my pocket and actually bought a double breasted gabardine suit at Henry Singers on my way through.

I graduated engineering school just before my 29th birthday in 1962, and to celebrate the occasion we drove to the Seattle World's Fair, in tandem with our friends Bob and Donna Westendorf. We both drove Volkswagen Beatles and had modified the seats to lay back, so we camped and slept in our cars. One evening after dark we pulled into a camping spot in Washington State, had our dinner and went to sleep. At some time in the night we woke up to the most incredible noise and bright lights;

we were camped beside a railroad track and a train was going by blowing its horn. I saw the ocean for the first time on that trip.

Mother Rosa receiving the Pioneer Citizen Award
Red Deer Chamber of Commerce, 1980

When we moved to Red Deer in 1954, Mother needed a job. She got a job at the Red Deer Hospital, in the kitchen washing pots and pans; you do what you have to do. Mother was a college graduate, Olds Agriculture College 1921, but she had never worked any place but on the farm. After college she had gone back to the farm to help with the milking and to do secretarial work for the Poet. In a short time Mother had a Nurse Aide Certificate and soon became the Ward Aide on the Operating room floor; they loved her and called her Bennie.

Chapter 26

The First Trip to Iceland

November, 1970

Dear Mother:

I have finally put together an account of our visit to Iceland. We called you from New York just before we boarded the plane around 10:00 p.m. on Saturday, May 2, 1970. It was the first jet flight for Loftleidir, Iceland's privately owned airline, and they were a bit disorganized as they had never carried so many passengers on one flight before. They are a very popular airline as their fares are well below the IATA fares.

Rosa Benediktson and her four children and their spouses, 1965.

Restless as a Viking

We arrived at the overseas airport at Keflavík around 6:00 am Sunday morning, earlier than we had expected because of the jet service. My first sightings of Iceland were particularly pleasing as it represented something I had wanted to do for a long time.

The weather was fresh with traces of snow on the ground but not really cold, much like the weather in Calgary the week we were at home. There were some patches of green grass around the terminal building. Some 20 of us hardier souls left the flight at Keflavík. The drive into Reykjavík through the old lava flows is a rather bleak experience. I could not help but wonder if it was the Icelanders or the Americans who picked this location for an international airport in those early days of World War II.

We checked into Hotel Borg, freshened up and went down for breakfast – a failure. After breakfast we all went to bed and slept until lunch time when we had a call from Guðmundur Benediktsson in the Prime Minister's office; Guðmundur is not related to Prime Minister Bjarni Benediktsson. As you know the Prime Minister and I have exchanged Christmas Cards since our meetings at Markerville in 1963. Last Christmas I mentioned that we planned to visit Iceland this year and he sent a note asking me to let him know when we were coming, which I did before we left Melbourne.

Guðmundur extended greetings from the Prime Minister and invited us to an official dinner at Hotel Borg the next evening. It was one of the functions in connection with the inauguration of the Búrfell Hydroelectric Plant and the Aluminum Reduction Plant located at Straumsvík between Keflavík and Reykjavík. The complex is owned 49% by Swiss interests and 51% by the Icelanders, financed by a West German bank.

I explained to Guðmundur that we had not brought formal clothes with us, but he insisted that it did not matter so I accepted. Needless to say we were the only ones in attendance in street clothes but it was all a great success. We went for a long walk around Reykjavík that after noon. That evening Audrey and I went to the Hotel Saga for dinner; the restaurant is at the top of the hotel with a fine view of the city and the harbour, and the food was excellent.

The next day we wanted to see something of the country side as Audrey, Susan and David were scheduled to fly to London on Tuesday morning to meet her family for the first time since she left London in 1945. I arranged for a rental car and discovered in the process that Icelanders are not early risers; nothing much happens before at least 9:00 a.m. I believe they stay up later than we do in the evenings, however, which is probably sensible because of the long summer days.

The next morning we took off in a rented Volkswagen for a tour of Þingvellir, the site of the ancient outdoor parliament, the Alþingi. It was a beautiful drive, particularly the section along the shores of Lake Þingvellir. We saw dozens of the long haired Icelandic sheep and the Icelandic horses. We stopped at the hotel in Hafnarfjörður and I ordered lunch in my broken Icelandic, which impressed the children. We had a delicious fish dinner starting with a rice in hot milk soup.

When we got back to Reykjavík, Audrey and I went shopping at one of the Íslenzkur heimilisiðnaður stores. We bought beautiful hand knit woolen sweaters for $12, etc. The sales lady knew your cousin Sigrún Stefánsdóttir, who you met and who also works at one of these stores. Unfortunately Sigrun was at home in the north because of a death in the family so we did not get to see her. After shopping Audrey went to get her hair done and I took the children out for dinner. While Audrey and I got ready for our state dinner party the children watched the guests arrive out of the hotel window, all in formal attire.

The Prime Minister and the President, Kristján Eldjárn, and their wives were in the receiving line. We met a lot of nice people, such as Sveinn and Helga Valfells, Guðmundur Benediktsson and the ex-President Ásgeir Ásgeirsson, whom we had met when he came to Markerville in 1961. As you no doubt know, Helga Valfells' father and Stephan G. were close friends. Their home was one of the two places that Stephan G. stayed at in Reykjavík when he visited Iceland in 1917.

When Sveinn Valfells learned of my plan to take Stevie to the north with me he insisted we go home with them after dinner to borrow parka coats for the trip, which we did. It was a late spring and cold in the north. The Valfells have a lovely home with beautiful furnishings. I was subsequently told that Sveinn was the richest man in Iceland at that time and if so it sits well on him. They are fine gracious people. They have three children, two boys and a girl. As I recall the girl has a PhD and teaches at a university in the USA, and the two boys are engineers. I believe the oldest has a PhD, is married and lives in Reykjavik, and the youngest is still studying in the USA.

It seems that Helga's father and Stephan G. had a scheme for testing a method of communicating after death. They both wrote letters and sealed them in an envelope. The first to die was to communicate what he had written to the other one who would verify it by opening and reading the letter. They have both died and the letters remain unopened. Helga brought out her father's letter and wanted me to open it, but I was a bit hesitant so she said we would open it on my next visit to Iceland, and if it is still there when I go back I will do that. In the meantime Sveinn had opened a 40 year old bottle of brenavin, and we had a couple of drinks.

On Tuesday morning, it was a short night for Audrey and I. Stevie and I drove them out to the airport and checked them on to Flugfélag, Iceland's state airline, on a direct flight to London. We later learned that they had a pleasant flight and arrived on time at London's Heathrow Airport, where they were met by Audrey's two sisters and her brother.

Stevie and I went back to the hotel, checked out, drove to the domestic airport in town, returned the rent car and checked onto a Flufélag flight to Akureyri to visit the Skagafjörður District where Stephan G. was from. We later learned that we could have flown directly to Sauðárkrókur in the Skagafjörður District but were pleased for the opportunity to see more of the country and the people.

We had met the ex-President Ásgeirsson's son and his American wife at the state dinner, and Ásgeirsson had mentioned that they would be at the airport this morning as his son and his wife were on the same flight to Akureyri. The son is a graduate of an American engineering school and was working on the construction of a diatomaceous earth plant at Lake Mývatn. When we met Ásgeirsson at the airport he introduced us to another passenger, Sigurður Björnsson, a bank manager from Húsavík; a small man of considerable authority. He immediately arranged window seats for both Stevie and I and explained the countryside to us as we flew over it. It was a clear day and the views were magnificent. When we arrived to Akureyri, Sigurður introduced us to the Airport Manager who offered to make onward arrangements for us. He reserved a room at the KEA Hotel for us, arranged for us to travel to Arnarstapi the next day by bus and to be picked up by car there for a tour. Arnarstapi is where Stephan G. left from in 1873 to immigrate to the New World, almost 100 years ago.

After we had checked into KEA we went for a walk around town where we met an American and his wife in one of the stores. Ray Bailey was from Clarion, Iowa and his son was stationed at Keflavík with the American air force. Ray was in the process of chartering a plane to fly to the Island of Grímsey and if the airstrip was dry they were going to land and have a look around. This would entitle them to a certificate attesting to the fact they had crossed the Arctic Circle. They invited us to join them, but as we had made arrangements to take a bus trip to a ski lodge overlooking the city of Akureyri and the Eyjafjörður District, we declined.

The views from the ski lodge were inspiring, the sea and snow exactly the blue and white colors in the Icelandic flag. I discovered a book in the reading room called *Vesturíslenzkar æviskrár* by Benjamín Kristjánsson that included a description of the Benediktson and Stephansson families complete with pictures, including one of myself. It was one of the first edition, printed in Akureyri, and I now have a copy of the somewhat modified third edition.

When we went down for breakfast the next morning they were announcing on the radio the news that Mt. Hekla had started erupting the previous evening. It had been dormant since 1947 and just now started to perform on the occasion of our visit. I had started school in the Markerville District at Hecla School, a possible connection.

We got Stevie's haircut as we waited for the bus, and the barber and I had such an excellent conversation in Icelandic that we almost missed our bus. He could speak no English but it was getting easier and easier for me to understand and be understood in Icelandic.

We met our American friends of the day before on the bus. They had made their trip to Grímsey Island and were going back to Reykjavík, about 280 miles by road; the weather was beautiful and the bus ride was delightful. The coastline of Iceland is a series of fjords, fingers of water between ridges of barren rocks. The level land on either side of the fingers of water is very fertile farm land. The pastures were turning green in the warm spring air, and the farms along the way appeared to be modern and well kept. The road was not the best as the frost was coming out of the ground and creating some soft spots. We found a milk truck bogged down in one of the soft spots with a friendly Esso tanker driver helping him out. After much organizing, shovelling, pushing and pulling we got the milk truck on his way again.

It turned out that the car waiting for us at Arnarstapi was not a rental car as I expected but a private car with a committee of three gentlemen who were sincerely interested in meeting some descendants of Stephan G. There was Guðmundur Guðmundsson, who was one of the leaders of the Youth Club that raised the money for the monument to Stephan G. at Arnastapi. He has lived in England but prefers this part of the world, the north coast of Iceland. He is a very intelligent, thoughtful man. Then there was Óskarsson who you met at Skagafjörður in 1953 when you were there to unveil the monument, a most amiable pleasant fellow. Our chauffeur was Flóvent Albertsson, who also chauffeured you around in 1953 and still has the coin that Stephan G. gave him for holding his horse on his return visit to Iceland in 1917.

We had lunch and then went for a tour of the district. We visited the old sod roofed church where Stephan G. was confirmed and that is now maintained as a historic site. From there we went to the monument. The most striking feature of the monument is that it is so much a part of its environment. It is in the style of the stone cairns erected along the roads in the early days to mark the way in the winter time when the country side is snow covered. It commands a magnificent view of the fjord, Skagafjörd, with Drangey Island clearly seen. We have enjoyed the painting of Drangey Island hanging in the living room of Stephansson House as long as I can remember. There is a legend that Drangey was a cow being led by a lady that was forbidden to look back but looked back and they were both turned into rocks.

Cenotaph of Stephan G. Stephansson
Arnarstapi, Iceland

We had coffee with the farmer who lives on the old farm site. It is not a prosperous farm, and the farmer has been known to say that if views were worth anything he would be a rich man. He is a keen horseman. I was told in Reykjavík that the men of Skagafjörður are noted for their love of wine, women and horses, a reasonable heritage I would say.

After coffee we drove into Sauðárkrókur with one stop at an old farm near a church south of the town that is maintained as a national memorial site. It is an enormous complex of the old board fronted sod houses, all furnished from the blacksmith shop to the nursery, which was very interesting for both Stevie and I. When we got to the town we had some more coffee at the home of Guðjón Ingimundarson, who has done much to preserve the memory of Stephan G. in the district. We met Eyþór Stefánsson the conductor at Guðjón's home. I understand that Eyþór is over 80, although he does not look a day over 50. We had a real Icelandic coffee with fancy creamed sandwiches and a dozen different kinds of cakes before we had to rush off to catch our plane back to Reykjavík.

We stayed at the City Hotel for our last two days, a moderately priced hotel with very nice people, as we found everywhere we went in Iceland. We had no sooner checked in when the phone rang. It was Kristinn Baldursson, Bjarni Benediktsson's cousin, the farmer on Stephan G.'s old homesite, whose wife's brother and father were close friends of Stephan G. His father was working in Winnipeg around the turn of the century when father started corresponding with Stephan G. They continued to correspond when he returned to Iceland and finally met when Stephan G. visited Iceland in 1917.

Kristinn offered to drive us out to see the Mt. Hekla eruption that evening and we accepted. He and his daughter drove us out to a point some distance from the eruption. We stood on a ridge overlooking a river and watched the red tongues of lava flowing down the mountainside and listened to the roar of the eruption. We were covered with volcanic dust before we left for Reykjavik, arriving around 3:00 a.m., another full day.

Friday, our last full day in Iceland, was a national holiday. Kristinn and his brother picked us up and took us to visit a friend of theirs, Gunnar Eggertsson. Gunnar, who has a lovely home on the sea, has studied Stephan G.'s work in considerable detail. We had a good visit including a few drinks of Armenian brandy. In our travels I learned to skol Icelandic style. They say scowl, not skol, and look the other person in the eye, a bit disconcerting at first, very personal. I also learned what a "hestskál" is. It is sort of a horse and buggy version of one for the road.

Family

From there we went to visit the Rev. Benjamín Kristjánsson, author of *Vestur-íslenzkar æviskrár*, in his lovely home, a good visit complete with Icelandic coffee and cakes. A most interesting person, Benjamín retired from a large congregation at Akureyri and is widely travelled. He has the largest private library I have ever seen. As we left he gave me an autographed copy of his book.

We went from there to Ásmundur Sveinsson's gallery. As luck would have it the sculptor was at home and in fact out in his yard when we arrived. We introduced ourselves, and he took us on a personalized tour of the grounds and gallery. I have never been so impressed by a single meeting with one person before. He was rather unkempt, as though he was too busy to worry about little things like his appearance, in his late seventies and still full of this tremendous enthusiasm for his work and life. He spoke only Icelandic and talked so fast I could not understand anything he said, but as I don't recall having to say anything during the course of the tour that really didn't matter. He told us what he called every piece of his work and the works were very appropriately named. There are a lot of them, and most of them are big. He uses a variety of materials ranging from mortar to old bath tubs. His perception and imagination are certainly not those of an ordinary man. He told me that he remembered Stephan G.'s visit to Iceland in 1917, but they did not meet because he was studying in Paris at the time. Before we left he gave me a small plaster copy of one of his works that he called *Man into Woman* that I hope to get larger copy of sometime.

On our way back to Kristinn's house we stopped at the Hotel Loftleidir and bought Stevie the "lundi", a stuffed puffin, that I had promised him, and there we ran into our American friends, the Baileys, once again and said our goodbyes. Incidentally, Susan's memento of Iceland was one of the fluffy sheep skins.

Kristinn and his wife took us out for dinner that evening to a restaurant called The Naust that specializes in Icelandic food. It is done up like an old Viking ship and the food and service was excellent. I had herring for an appetizer, three kinds, followed by hangikjöt, then skyr and coffee, absolutely delicious.

After dinner Stevie went to bed as it was quit late and Kristinn and his wife took me for a last tour of Reykjavík. I saw parts of the city that I had not seen before. It was after 10:00 p.m. but still light, and I can remember looking out to sea over Reykjavík Harbour. The water was dead calm, which is apparently unusual, and the sea and the sky were exactly the same shade of blue-grey. You could not tell where the water ended and the sky began.

The next morning we were up bright and early to catch the bus to Keflavík where we boarded a Flugfélag flight to Glasgow, connecting to a BEA flight to London where Audrey and her sister Irenie met us. The visit to Iceland meant a lot to me. It represented something I had wanted to do for some time and I felt very much a part of the country and very in tune with the people, as Audrey did in England. These were wonderful experiences for all of us. As Guðmundur Benediktsson said, these 200,000 Icelanders share many things that are becoming more precious every day. They have clean air, water, countryside to expand to, untapped resources and the opportunity to combine the best of the old and new worlds.

Our vacation was filled with a series of coincidences that provided just what we wanted when we needed it. We recently heard the sad news that Bjarni Benediktsson, his wife and a grandchild were burned to death in their summer cottage. I only met him on two occasions, but I feel that I have lost a good friend and am grateful that we visited Iceland before this tragedy occurred.

Chapter 27

Our Summer Vacation 1995

The summer of 1995 was varied and action packed. Adriana's boys, Lavan and Jonathan, arrived the second week of June when they got out of school in Atlanta. Lavan has since gone on to become a cyber genius in marketing. Johnathan, having graduated in Fashion Design from MIT followed by two additional years of scholarship studies, one year in a coutier school in Rome, went on to work in the fashion industry in New York. Their older brother Alfredo has a car sales business in Gainesville, Georgia.

Adriana's mother, Elvira Kroes, arrived from Bogota, Colombia, in the third week of June and Monica, her daughter who lives with us in Canada, left for Atlanta in the first week of July. Monica who is not only very attractive is super smart and went on to graduate Cum Laude in business from Georgia State University. Adriana spent the summer entertaining and housekeeping and working in the yard.

I was out of the country on business for two weeks, returning in time to watch the Stampede Parade with them. We both enjoyed showing Elvira our way of life. Before they all left I took them on a "camping" trip to Nordegg, a 1920s coal mining town west of Red Deer. I wanted the boys to do at least one camping trip. Actually, we stayed in a hostel at Nordegg and on our return trip we stopped at Stephansson House.

On the second of August we put the boys on a plane to Atlanta and flew to New York where we spent two nights at the apartment of a friend from Amerada Hess days, Lambros Lambros. I had some business meetings, Adriana did some shopping and we had two excellent dinners. One dinner was with Lambros Lambros and Philip Herrera, originally from Guatemala, and his

Al, Adriana, Monica and Johnathan

wife, a Colombian. Herrera was a Harvard class mate of Lambros'. The other special dinner was with Bryan Lawrence and his wife Betsey. Both took us to Italian restaurants, seemingly a favorite venue for New Yorkers.

On Friday afternoon we drove out to Nick and Judy Trynin's place on Shelter Island in a rented car. It was hot. New York was setting a record for consecutive 100°F days. At the Trynin's we ate lobster at home on Friday night, and on Saturday we watched the inaugural polo game of the reactivated Bridgehampton Polo Club. Peter Brown's White Birch team with Argie 10 goaler Mariano Aguire went down to defeat at the hands of Adam Lindeman's Cellular Farm team made up of an Argie, two Americans and a Canadian. Peter Brown was responsible for the reactivation of the club. That night we dined at the Trynin's golf club, and the next day we drove to Kennedy where we boarded Icelandair for Reykjavík. A daily service leaving Kennedy at 8:00 p.m., the flight arrives at Keflavík at 6:00 a.m. with a four hour time change.

In June I had called an old family friend, Dr. Finnbogi Guðmundsson. Finnbogi was Associate Professor of Icelandic language and literature in the University of Manitoba, Winnipeg from 1951 to 1956, and later became the Director of the National Library of Iceland in Reykjavík from 1964 to 1994. Finnbogi has had a long standing interest in my grandfather and has edited three volumes of *Selected Letters to Stephan G. Stephansson* and published seven articles on the poet translated into English. I had not seen or talked to Finnbogi since 1980 when I stopped over in Reykjavík for a weekend en route from New York to London. When I introduced myself on the telephone to Finnbogi in June of this year he said, "Are you coming this summer?" I then sent him our itinerary and he was there to meet us.

We collected our luggage, loaded it into Finnbogi's small car and drove to his house in Hafnarfjörður where we had breakfast. I remembered the house from 1980. Finnbogi's daughter, Helga, then a student, had given us a private concert of Chopin on the piano. Since then, she had gone to Holland for graduate studies in music and met and married a fellow musician, a very successful American Dutch jazz musician. They had one daughter, Rosa, and then divorced and Helga returned to Iceland. Finnbogi's wife, a medical doctor, passed away in 1984. After breakfast Finnbogi delivered us to the Hotel Saga, very nice albeit, as most things are in Iceland today, somewhat expensive.

Finnbogi picked us up again at 2:00 p.m. and took us on a tour of Reykjavík. First we walked to the Icelandic Arnamagnean Manuscript Institute that houses Iceland's old manuscripts. The Sagas and Eddas are a notable chapter in the history of world culture, and the manuscripts which preserve them are precious monuments to the Icelandic people. The director of the Institute, Stefán Karlsson, and by the way a distant cousin of mine, met us and explained the workings of the Institute. We then visited the City Gallery, Ásgrimur Jónsson's Gallery, Ásmundur Sveinsson's Ásmundur Gallery as well as the garden of sculptor Einar Jónsson, where many of his works are exhibited. This we topped off with a swim in one of the outdoor pools that Iceland is famous for, Seltjarnarnes.

On our way back to the Hotel Saga we stopped at Kringlan, a very large, modern shopping mall that is complete with a Hard Rock Cafe. That evening we dined at Skólabrú, an excellent restaurant in the city centre, with Finnbogi and Ingólfur Guðbrandsson, the Director of Prima Travel Ltd. Ingólfur was a conductor of considerable note before and during the time he has operated the travel agency. He has conducted internationally, including in the United Kingdom, Spain and Italy. Ingólfur arranged our booking at the Hotel Saga, arranged for a rental car to drive to the north and advised Hjalti Pálsson, Director of Safnahúsið, Faxatorg, at Sauðárkrókur that we were coming. I had expressed a desire to stay on a horse farm in Iceland like our bed and breakfasts and to ride an Icelandic horse, and this had also been arranged for at Varmilækur, the farm of Björn Sveinsson.

On Tuesday, Finnbogi took us on a tour of the new National Library building, conveniently located near the Hotel Saga. The library was opened on December 1, 1994, consolidating the National Library of Iceland and the University Library and the culmination of Finnbogi's 30 years as a Director. It is both beautiful and functional. At the end of our tour, we went into a controlled environment vault where interesting old papers are kept, and a curator brought out materials held under the name of Stephan G. Stephansson, which included a number of letters and articles. Finnbogi then treated us to lunch at the library's cafeteria where we enjoyed cod as it is consumed by the major-

Family

ity of Icelanders for lunch each day, steamed, with melted butter and accompanied by boiled potatoes and a vegetable: very good. After lunch we visited the Pearl, a most interesting frame and glass bubble on top of three large hot water storage tanks on a hill overlooking the city. After a stop at the Nordic House in Reykjavík, Finnbogi left us at our hotel. That evening Adriana and I dined upstairs in the dining room of the Hotel Saga. The Icelandic salmon steaks and Icelandic lamb are just incredibly good. We had to wait as the dining room was full of tourists from Europe and the Orient. The next morning, Þorvaldur from the A.G. Bilaleiga car rental agency delivered our four wheel drive Subaru and Stefán Jörundsson arrived to act as our tour guide for the day. Stefán is the brother of Guðrún Jörundsdóttir, married to Dr. Hallgrímur Benediktsson, the resident pathologist at the Foothills Hospital in Calgary. We had a wonderful tour.

First we visited the plant at the geothermal center at Nesjavellir, some 50 kilometers east of Reykjavík. The plant is enormous and immaculate. The history of the development of geothermal energy in Iceland starting in 1928 is really the history of geothermal engineering. The National Energy Authority has a geothermal university that trains engineers and geologists from around the world, under the overall coordination of the United Nations.

We then visited Þingvellir, home of the world's first parliament, starting in 930 A.D. Here the chieftains from across the country would meet once per year to make law and resolve problems. After a coffee at the local hotel, we drove on to Geysir area, home of the original geyser after which all geysers are named. Here geysers spout every few minutes.

After dinner we went on to Gullfoss, very beautiful, and then into the town of Hveragerdi, which has its own geyser and a large tent-covered shopping center. We drove past a church in Eyrarbakki that Stefán and Guðrún's father had designed, and the three of us had dinner at the Þrír Frakkar Hjá Úlfari, an excellent fish restaurant in Reykjavík.

Next morning Thursday, August 10, coincidentally the day that Stephan G. died in 1927, we checked out of the Hotel Saga

113

and drove to the Skagafjörður District in the north, with stops to enjoy the view, to have lunch at the Hotel in Blönduós and to enjoy the monument to Stephan G. at Arnarstapi created by Ríkarður Jónsson. The monument was unveiled by my mother Rosa in 1953 on the occasion of the 100th Anniversary of the birth of Stephan G. on a farm called Kirkjuhóll, not far away.

At the town of Sauðárkrókur, we went directly to the Safnahúsið, Faxatorg, to meet the Director, Hjalti Pálsson. Hjalti described the purpose of the Safnahúsið. As I understand it, the Safnahúsiðis sort of a town hall, library and custodian of the district artifacts. At that moment it housed in the main exhibit room a joint exhibition by the National Archives and the National Museum prepared for the 50th Anniversary of the Republic of Iceland in 1994. Traditionally the story starts in 1830 with the July Revolution in France, which sent a message to the absolutist states of Europe, including Denmark. The independence movement culminated with a national referendum on May 20, 1944 that voted 95% to institute a republic. Bessastadir, previously the residence of the Danish Governor is now the official residence of the President of Iceland.

Hjalti gave me photocopies of the record of Stephan G.'s birth on October 3, 1853 and a record of Stephan G.'s confirmation June 10, 1867. The pastor had commented that he was a good learner. Hjalti also showed us the letters they hold in the archives from Stephan G. to various friends in the district, very moving.

After this, Hjalti took us on a tour of Sauðárkrókur, a town of some 3,000 inhabitants. It stands at the foot of the mountain Tindastóll, which was the namesake of a one roomed school east of Markerville where I graduated Grade 9 in 1947. The famous island of Drangey rising out of the water over 500 feet can be seen out on the fjord. We proceeded to the home of a local farmer, Þorsteinn Ásgrímsson, whose wife, Ingibjörg Sigurðardóttir, is my fourth cousin.

It seems that Stephan G.'s grandfather, Hannes Þorvaldsson had two families, one legitimate and one illegitimate. We are of the legitimate family; Ingibjórg is of the illegitimate side. We had coffee and an incredible selection of sweets at their home and met a lot of relatives, including Margrét Björk Andrésdóttir, Aðalsteinn Júlíusson, Ólöf Þorsteinsdóttir, Sigurbjörg Sigurðardóttir and Magnús Jónasson.

After coffee we went across country to see Kirkjuhóll where Stephan G. was born and then back to the farm at Arnarstapi where he lived with his parents when they left the Skagafjörður District for Mjóidalur, the farm of my Grandmother Helga's parents near Mýri in the Bárðardalur Valley. Helga and Stephan G. were cousins. The old farmhouses at both Kirkjuhóll and Víðimýrarsel are gone, but the markings in the ground are still obvious. We cousins stood on the old house site to have our picture taken on the day that Stephan G. died 68 years before by the farmer who now owns the land. The farmer said that he writes poetry, when he has time, inspired by the monument which he can see from is window. We stopped at Víðimýrarkirkja, a turf church from the last century, one of the oldest in the country. While Þorsteinn attended to the chores of his dairy farm and Hjalti went to pick up his wife, we went to our guest house, a Hestasport farm guesthouse near Varmahlid.

The farm is operated by Björn Sveinsson, no English, and his charming wife, an accomplished musician who speaks perfect English. Saurðárkrókur is known for its fine horses, of which this farm has about one hundred, and it's beautiful ladies. When we arrived a young lady showed us our room and explained that she was the *au pair*, from Germany, although she looked Icelandic, and that the lady of the house was away conducting a concert.

We went back to the hotel in Varmahlíð, where all of our new-found cousins had gathered with Hjalti and his wife for dinner. We had the best lamb I have ever tasted, and that is saying a lot from someone who was raised as an Icelander and who lived many years in Australia. We had a delightful evening, then back to our farm guest house. I must say that on this visit I saw no evidence of the excessive use of alcohol Icelanders have a reputation for. In fact I saw only very modest consumption, both privately and publicly.

In the morning around 8:00 a.m. our hostess had an incredible breakfast waiting for us. What a spread. She and her husband had been out putting up hay since 5:00 a.m. After breakfast she had one of her nieces tack up two horses and take me on a ride. I had always wanted to ride one of these famous five gaited Icelandic horses, the most famous gait being a very fast trot called the tölt. We crossed fields, hills and streams and valleys. It was very pleasant. My guide was a young, tall, very attractive, quiet, bilingual young lady who obviously loved animals; our hostess was also tall like a Viking. The guide's face would light up like a lamp when she petted the horses or the dogs.

From the horse farm we drove to the Glaumbær Folk Museum between Varmahlíðand Sauðárkrókur. Glaumbær is an old turf farmhouse that was lived in until 1947. The atmosphere is so real that you almost become one of the household. An interesting feature in Glaumbær is that Snorri Þorfinnsson lived and is buried there. Snorri, born in 1002, was the first European born in North America. Snorri's father led an expedition to America and wintered there for three years with his wife and others after Leifur Eríksson discovered America in 1000 A.D.

From Glaumbær we drove to Hola in Hjaltadalur. Around the turn of the century, Stephan G. organized a school for his and other children in the District and called it Hola. At Markerville, Hola school, near Stephansson House, is still used as a community centre. In Iceland, Hólar is one of the great historic sites. The cathedral at Hólar is the seat for the Bishop in the north, a very pretty area complete with an agricultural college.

From Hólar, we drove to Akureyri and checked into the Hotel Harpa, three kilometers south of Akureyri. After we checked-in, I called Ingólfur Ásgeir Jóhannesson, another new cousin who had called me at the Hotel Saga in Reykjavík when he heard we were coming. Ingólfur has a doctorate from the University of Wisconsin in education and recently obtained a seat at the University of Akureyri.

Inglófur later sent me two papers on educational reform that he had published that are so complicated and academic that they are paralyzing; he must have a very high IQ. We visited and arranged our weekend, this being Friday. We agreed to tour Lake

Mývatn, noted for its deposits of diatomaceous earth, and the Bárðardalur Valley to Mýri, where grandmother's family lived on Saturday, and to meet family at the Hotel Harpa for afternoon tea on Sunday. The family matriarch, Helga Kristjánsdóttir, would contact various relatives to come to tea. My mother, Rosa, spent time with Helga when she visited the north in 1953. Before we parted Ingólfur recommended a restaurant for dinner.

We started our tour on Saturday morning in good time. Ingólfur was an excellent guide and travelling companion. First we stopped at Goðafoss then on to Lake Mývatn. The area around Mývatn is unique in the world. The bird and plant life are unique. There are all manner of volcanic craters, unusual lava formations, colorful geothermal areas with boiling mud pits and black sands. We did the walking tour of Dimmuborgir and saw the craggy "Black Castles" of old lava flows and Kirkjan, the cave called the church. After Mývatn we drove to Grjótagjá, the lava ridge with the underground pools. Until 1977, when there was an eruption at Leirhnúkur, the pools were used for bathing, but since that time the water has been too hot. We did our Icelandic customary afternoon swim at the swimming pool at Skútustaðir.

In the afternoon we drove down the Bárðardalur Valley to a cousin's home, Jóhann, a farmer. We are related through Helga Kristjánsdóttir on my grandmother's side. Grandmother was also named Helga. As you can imagine we had coffee and cakes. The lady of the house had a French mother, and one of their daughters and her husband had adopted a Colombian orphan. The grandparents were very proud of their adopted grandchild and tried to convince us that he looked a little Icelandic because of his high cheekbones. Jóhann looked very like my cousins, Jack or Cecil or Lorne Stephansson. He spoke such exact Icelandic that I understood a lot of what he said. Ingólfur commented on his command of the Icelandic language. Jóhann came with us and we drove to Mýri, the area where Helga's family had lived. After saying our goodbyes, we returned to Akureyri. Adriana and I had a great dinner at a restaurant across from a well-used soccer field.

The next morning we went for a walk around town with a little shopping at the few shops that were open. In the afternoon Helga arrived with about two dozen relatives. It was a very pleasant time. Ingólfur did the translating and drew the family tree with Helga's help. They all left after a decent interval. We said our goodbyes to all and to Ingólfur, then checked out of the hotel and drove back to Reykjavík. Returning to the Hotel Saga was like coming home.

I did not take the time to pursue my father's roots in Iceland on this trip. I look forward to doing that on my next trip to Iceland. From what I know it sounds very interesting. Grandfather and grandmother came from the Húnavatnssýsla District in Northwestern Iceland, grandfather was Benedikt Guðmundsson from Miðfjörður and grandmother was Ingibjörg Guðmundsdóttir from Urriðaá. What is interesting is that this is the District that Grettir the Strong came from around the year 1100; maybe we are related.

As I understand it, Grettir was not easy to live with. As a young man he had numerous conflicts and left the country to live abroad for a time. When he returned an unfortunate accident occurred, a building caught fire and burned down and some people lost their lives. Rightly or wrongly, Grettir was blamed for the accident and was labelled an outlaw. In Iceland, at that time, a man so labelled could be killed by anyone. If he survived for 20 years, he was freed of the outlaw label and could rejoin society. Grettir lived on the island of Drangey that rises vertically out of the fjord at Skagafjordur. The only access to the plateau at the top of the island was a rope ladder. In the nineteenth year of his life as an outlaw, his servant forgot to pull the rope ladder up one night. some men went to the top, captured Grettir and killed him. Grettir's Saga has been translated and published. I look forward to reading it and to learning more about my father's family.

Monday we explored Main Street Reykjavík in the morning, and in the afternoon Finnbogi took me to the offices of Guðmundur Pálmason, Director of the Geotechnical Division of the National Energy Authority. Guðmundur introduced me to one of his staff, Karl Gunnarsson, a geophysicist, who had studied and worked in the oil and gas industry in North America. This was interesting but more of a social call as in my opinion the prospects for discovery of oil or gas in or around Iceland are not great as the geological setting is too "new".

That evening we dined alone together at the Skólabrú, which we had enjoyed so much our first evening in Reykjavik. On Tuesday, we had a lovely lunch and visit with Margarét Andrésdóttir, one of the cousins we met at Sauðárkrókur. In the evening we had dinner with Heiður Vigfúsdóttir and her husband, Dr. Birgir Gudjonsson. Heidur is the daughter of Sigrún Stefánsdóttir, who my mother Rosa stayed with in 1953. Rosa and Sigrún continued to correspond by mail; mother was a great letter writer.

Birgir holds a graduate degree in internal medicine from Yale, the first foreign student to achieve this, and has a general practice specializing in internal medicine. Birgir has another first. He is one of 75 Directors of the World Athletic Association and had just returned from the World Athletic competition in Sweden. Some ten years earlier his eldest son was on the Icelandic Olympic track and field team in the Olympic competition with Birgir who threw the hammer. This was the first father and son team in Olympic history to that time. They have a fine and interesting family. The son now has a PhD in Archeology and lives in Chicago, one daughter has a PhD in mathematics and another plans to be a writer. We had a wonderful evening together, a great last night in Iceland. The next morning we left the hotel very early to fly to London.

On our last day in Iceland, August 15, I was interviewed by a reporter for the *Morgunblaðið*, and an article, with a picture of Adriana and I, was published in the paper on Sunday, August 20, 1995.

The air terminal at Keflavík is beautiful and has been named the best airport in Europe. The duty free shops are well appointed and stocked. The flight to Heathrow is less than three hours. As we walked from the arrival gate to the luggage pick-up area at Heathrow two things became apparent: first, the weather in London was unusually hot; and second, that had not discouraged visitors to London. In fact it was the hottest summer in London's 350 years of recording temperatures. It was so hot that people in the UK stayed at home and took their summer vacations at the British beaches, to the dismay of the tour operators.

We picked up our luggage and proceeded to the Hotel Plaza on Hyde Park by taxi and were all checked in shortly after noon. Our vacation plans in the UK were very casual; we wanted to see some shows and saw *Sunset Boulevard* and *Forever Tango* (both great experiences), to buy some silverware and china (we bought a set of silver ware and a set of Royal Doulton china), and to do London and the British countryside as typical tourists (we did day trips to both Windsor and Dover by train). In London we saw Buckingham Palace, the Tower of London, Big Ben, Soho, shopped on Regent Street, visited the Royal Academy of Arts, which was featuring works by Monet and Gauguin, shopped at Harrods and Selfridges.

We became expert at riding "the tube". Adriana had been scheduled to go to university in London (her father went to Cambridge), but instead she got married after high school. She had been to London twice before, the first time as a guest of her father's uncle, since deceased, who had owned a successful perfume factory there. We packed so much in that week that we were ready to leave, and on Wednesday, August 23, 1995 we flew from London to New York with a change of planes in Keflavík. Europe had been wonderful, but we were glad to be back in North America and checked in to the Plaza Hotel.

On Thursday I visited Bryan Lawrence exactly three weeks after my last visit. The day was spent shopping; I bought my fourth and last Remington bronze, *Coming through the Rye*, from my friends at Caesars Plaza Inc., next to the Plaza Hotel. Through the years, I have purchased *The Outlaw*, *The Bronco Buster* and *The Mountain Man*. I arranged for them to ship it to Calgary as, unlike the first three, it weighs too much to take as luggage.

I also picked up my clarinet from the International Woodwind & Brass Center on West 48th Street. I had left it for recorking and repairs on my last visit to New York some five months earlier.

Family

My dear old mother gave me the clarinet in 1947 so I could take music lessons in Grade 10. In spite of the excellent instruction from Mr. Merta, at the Red Deer Composite High School, about the only thing I could play after a year of instruction was "The Lucky Old Sun". It is a fine wooden French piece, unlike the new ones which are almost all made of plastic. I have since given it to my nephew, Bill Bourne, who had it on loan for some ten years and went on to win a Juno award, but not on the clarinet. That evening we flew from New York to Calgary with a change of planes in Toronto. We took a taxi to the office where I picked-up my car and drove home: a great vacation.

Chapter 28

Who was Guðríður Þorbjarnardóttir?

Guðríður Þorbjarnardóttir accompanied the Norse explorers who sailed to the shores of North America in their open sailing ships over one thousand years ago. She and her husband Þorfinnur Karlsefni were following in the wake of Leifur Eríksson, who was the first European to discover the North American continent. During the first of three winters spent in Vinland at a place they called Straumsvik, she gave birth to a son that they named Snorri, the first European child born in North America. In his recent book, *Vinlandsgátan* or *The Vineland Puzzle*, author Páll Bergþorsson analyses the Vinland voyages from the Saga writings, considering weather, ocean currents and researching the areas around the Gulf of St. Lawrence, and concludes that Straumsvik was located where St. John, New Brunswick stands today.

Guðríður was born in Iceland at Laugarbrekka in the West of Iceland on the Snæfellsnes Peninsula. She travelled to Greenland with her father and settled there, where she met and married Þorsteinn, Erík the Red's son. *The Greenlander's Saga* tells us that she and a crew left Greenland for Vinland in one ship but became lost at sea as a result of bad weather. On their return to Greenland that fall Þorstein fell ill and died. Guðríður later married Þorfinnur Karlsefni, a trader from Skagafjörður. With a crew of 140 on three ships they sailed to Vinland and spent three years exploring and attempting to establish themselves there. However, the Indians, who they called Skraelings, became increasingly hostile towards them so they had to abandon the country and sail back to Greenland, taking with them a cargo of riches from the new land.

Guðríður and her family subsequently returned to Iceland where they bought a farm at Glaumbær in Skagafjörður. Following the death of her second husband, the Sagas tell us that Guðríður travelled to Europe and made a pilgrimage to Rome where she reported on the New World. Iceland converted to Christianity, Catholicism, in the year 1000. They were Pagan prior to that. Later the vast majority of Icelanders converted to Lutheranism. She then returned to Iceland and lived a cloistered life at the church built there by her son Snorri. She was an explorer of renown and undoubtedly the most travelled lady of those ages. She was a fine representative of these resourceful, adventurous, seafaring people who led the way in discovering, mapping and exploring the New World, long before other Europeans ventured that far into the unknown.

A statue at the National Gallery of Iceland commemorating Snorri and Guðríður was sculpted by the Icelandic artist Ásmundur Sveinsson. A copy of that statue was presented to the Museum at Glaumbær in Skagafjörður as a gift from North Americans of Icelandic descent and unveiled by President Vigdís Finnbogadóttir on July 10, 1994.

Chapter 29

Icelanders – They Are Everywhere

Icelanders are everywhere. After 1,000 years of settlement by the Norsemen they are a nation of 300,000 people, and it is impressive how they have moved around. I have lived in nine countries, and everywhere I have lived I have looked for and generally found Icelanders.

In the late 1960s I lived in Melbourne, Australia; there I found an Icelander, Finnsson. He had been sent to a Boy Scout Jamboree in Australia as a young man and never left. Finnsson had a fishing boat and fished mussels and shell fish in Port Phillip Bay at Melbourne. He was married to an interesting British lady who even at that time was what we call a "Granola", concerned with organic foods and very occupied with developing a type of healthy bread. I learned years later that her bread had become popular and that she was very successful financially.

We moved to Sydney after that where one of my mother's Icelandic friend's daughters from Markerville lived. She had married a successful Australian oil man, Darren Wales. From Australia Exxon transferred us to Djakarta, Indonesia, where I met two Icelanders working for the World Food and Health Administration, based in Rome, Italy. They were installing small freezing plants for fish in appropriate coastal parts of Indonesia.

In Ottawa I became friends with a Saskatchewan born Icelandic Canadian engineer, Al Arnason, who worked for the Department of the Environment there, and later while working for Aramco in Saudia Arabia, in the mid 1970's, I met an Icelander, Hermannsson, working in Aramco's Maintenance Department.

After that I spent quite a number of years in South America where, curiously, I do not recall meeting any Icelanders. A few years later, while looking at an oil deal in Senegal, West Africa, I heard two men in the restaurant in our hotel speaking Icelandic. They told me they were pilots for a charter airline.

While driving from Atlanta to Calgary some years ago, I crossed into Canada from North Dakota, travelled some distance north and then turned and drove straight west to Alberta. When I arrived at a town called Baldur, I stopped for gasoline. As the attendant was filling the tank I went into the office to wait for him where I noticed a poster advertising Valgardsson's farm auction. When the attendant came in, I said, "I see you have some Icelanders around here." He replied, "Yes, would you like some."

A very special encounter was meeting Arni Thorsteinson, who started life as a Saskatchewan farm boy, at a cocktail party at the Banff Centre some years ago, the start of a very pleasant friendship. Arni emailed me the next winter to accept my invitation if he ever came to visit San Miguel de Allende to come to our home for a glass of wine and watch the sun go down. Arni said, "Get some food in. We will have dinner with you. We are ten couples. Oh by the way, we would like to meet some interesting local people," very Icelandic. I replied, "Okay." We had a very interesting, fun evening; interesting local people are not hard to find in San Miguel.

When I retired to fascinating San Miguel it took me over a year to find an Icelander, but I did. Cal Nordman has an ice-cream parlour and Italian coffee house here, was a medalist pistol shooter some years ago, and is an Icelandic-Canadian from Brandon, Manitoba. We now have a third Icelander here: Gerður Kristjánsdóttir, a born in Iceland, Icelander living in Boulder, Colorado with a second home here. The beautiful wool sweaters labelled Iceland that are sold in upscale shops around the world are from Gerður's business.

My classic encounter with an Icelander was when I discovered that one of the Canadian "Snow Birds" at our bridge club in San Miguel de Allende, Professor Kenneth Graham, PhD, was the grandson of the brother of K.N. Julius, the Icelandic American humorist poet. K.N. was a friend of my grandfather, Stephan

G. Stephansson, and in fact we have a photo of them together. What are the odds of two grandchildren of two of Iceland's poets playing bridge at the same club in a small town in Central Mexico 100 years later?

Icelanders are everywhere.

Chapter 30

Christinnson-Stephansson Cemetery

Stephan G. Stephansson and his brother-in-law, Kristinn Christ-innson, arrived in Alberta from North Dakota with their families in the summer of 1889 and settled on opposite sides of the Medicine River three miles north of Markerville. Siglaug Christinnson and Stephan were brother and sister, and their mother, Gutðbjórg Hannesdóttir, lived with Stephan.

Crossing the Medicine.
circa 1900

In 1904 the Hola Bridge was built across the Medicine between the two farms to provide access to settlements in the West Country, and Hola School was built at the crossing to provide for children of settlers on both sides of the river.

The Christinnsons had two sons, Stephan (Steve) and Hannes (Frost), and one daughter, Lilia. In 1905 while working for the

The Hola Bridge
Medicine River, Alberta, 1921

Eau Claire Lumber Company in Calgary, Steve contracted typhoid fever and passed away. While Steve was sick and dying he kept repeating that he wanted to go home, so in fact the family took the body home and interred him on the banks of the Medicine River near the Christinnson farm home. This was how the Christinnson-Stephansson cemetery was started.

The cemetery was first surveyed in 1909 and then subsequently resurveyed in 1952 and 1988. It has never been a public cemetery, always reserved for the Christinnson and Stephansson families. On July 16, 1909, Gestur Stephansson was killed by lightening while crossing a wire fence on the Stephansson farm, 16 years of age in July 1909, and became the second member of the family to be interred there. The third person to be interred there was Stephan G.'s mother, Guðbjörg, who passed away on January 18, 1911. Subsequent family members to be interred there prior to 1936 were Lillian Johnson in 1926, Kristinn Christinnson in 1926, the poet, Stephan G. in 1927 and Siglaug Christinsson in 1936.

The Christinnsons had a board fence built around the cemetery. It was nicely done with the Icelandic words "*Komin Heim*",

128

meaning "arrived home" above the gate. In 1934, the family and some friends and neighbors built a new fence around the perimeter with concrete posts and two strands of chain which stands to this day, some 80 years later. The posts, which have two holes in each post to string the chain through, were made in Red Deer by August Asmundson, a family friend. Steve Stephansson, Baldur's eldest son, transported the posts from Red Deer to the cemetery.

Tony Kressman from Sylvan Lake was hired to construct a cenotaph at the resting place of the poet, Stephan G. Stephansson, and the gate posts for the cemetery in 1936. Steve and Edwin Stephansson, cousins, and Ofiegur Sigurdsson, a close friend of the poet's, hauled stones from various places in the Hola and Centreville Districts to the cemetery for Kressman to use. The project was funded by contributions from neighbors and Icelanders in Canada, United States and Iceland. Ofieger Sigurdsson received the contributions and coordinated the project, which was unveiled on July 19, 1936 with over 200 people in attendance. This undertaking was remarkable when one considers it was done in the height of the Great Depression, without any public funding.

The cemetery was initially covered with trees and brush that had to be cleared for each of the graves. In the mid-forties the family had the plot cleared by a local landscape gardener called "Cabbage" Andersen. For whatever reason the grass did not catch well and it took considerable extra work over several years to establish the fine grassed area as it is today.

Since 1936, family members interred in the Christinnson-Stephansson Cemetery have been Sam Johnson, 1939; Helga, wife of the poet, December 12, 1940; their daughter Stephanie, who died in a car accident on the day of her mother's interment; Sigurleana, Baldur's wife, on October 29, 1942; Sigurdur Vilberg Benediktson, Rosa's husband, on November 18, 1942; Gestur, Baldur's youngest son on July 13, 1944; Baldur on June 17, 1949; the ashes of Jakob, the youngest son, in March, 1958; on September 11, 1962, Frost Christinnson; on July 9, 1960, Siggi Sigurdsson; his wife, Jenny, daughter of the poet, on June 28,

1969; Arni Bardal, beside his wife Stephanie, on May 21, 1971; on June 15, 1973, Steve Stephansson; his brother Cecil on January 22, 1977; his brother-in-law, August Seigfried on March 19, 1981 and his wife Lillie ; the ashes of the poet's youngest daughter, Rosa, spread on her husband's grave in 1995; as were the ashes of their two youngest sons, Theodor, 1990, and Conrad, 1992.

A partial list of the distinguished guests who have visited the Christinnson-Stephansson Cementery to pay their respects to Stephan G. Stephansson over the years includes His Excellency, Ásgeir Ásgeirsson, President of Iceland, on September 20, 1961; Dr. Bjarni Benediktsson, Prime Minister of Iceland, on August 7, 1964; Her Excellency, Vigdís Finnbogadóttir, President of Iceland, the first lady elected as President of any republic world-wide, on July 20, 1991; His Excellency, Ólafur Ragnar Grímsson, President of Iceland, on August 20, 1999.

The Christinnson-Stephansson Cemetery represents a very significant tie to the pioneer heritage that Albertans share. It is a particularly important site for the global body of academics and intellectuals who know of and respect the memory of Stephan G. Stephansson, the "Poet of the Rocky Mountains".

The descendants of Kristinn and Siglaug Christinnson and Stephan and Helga Stephansson feel strongly about their heritage in this part of Alberta. They carry out the maintenance and consider the Christinnson-Stephansson Cemetery an option for family members.

Edwin Stephansson and Stephan Benediktson, June, 2002

Family

Attachment 1

August 30, 2007

To: Premier of Alberta and Reeve of the Municipal District

Dear Sirs,

The almost complete lack of consideration for Western Canada's historic treasures continues to amaze me. I am from the Markerville District, west of Red Deer, Alberta, but no longer reside in Canada. It was recently brought to my attention that the bridge over the Medicine River in the Hola District near Markerville was removed, at significant cost and in spite of the community's objections.

That bridge was built over 100 years ago and represented major progress for the community of hard working homesteaders. The bridge provided year around safe access to the districts being developed on the west side of the river. The community asked that it be left in place. It could have been used for decades as a walking bridge. Now this historic enclave of Stephansson House, the Hola School and the Cristinsson-Stephansson Cemetery is once again separated by a river with no way to cross without traveling several miles around by car. The bridge beautifully illustrated the design and style of bridges of that period. The design and appearance were in keeping with and of the same period as the house, the school and the cemetery. The bridge, as it was constructed at that time and what the bridge meant to the community at that time, was historically irreplaceable.

Yours truly, Stephan V. Benediktson

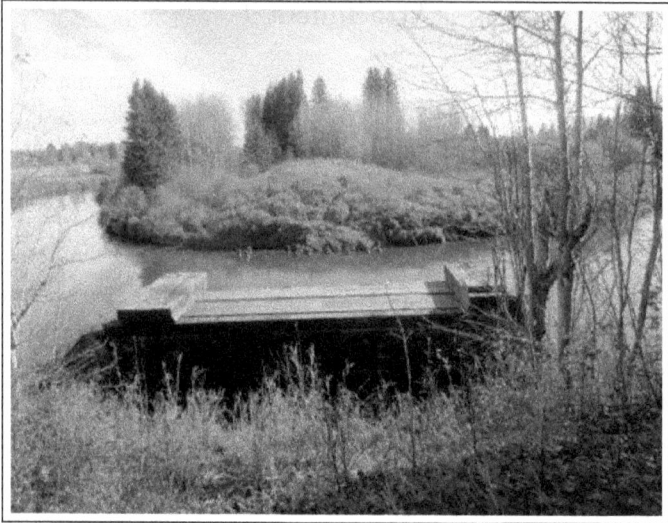

Looking East at Hola Bridge today.

Attachment 2

August 7, 2014

To: Premier of Alberta and Reeve of the Municipal District

Dear Sirs,

In 2006 the historic Hola Bridge, constructed across the Medicine River in 1911, was removed, despite objections from the community. That bridge provided a connection between Stephansson House, the historic Hola School and the Christinnson-Stephansson Cemetery, where Stephansson is interred.

132

Looking West at Hola Bridge today.

When the Hola Bridge was built it represented major progress for a community of hard working homesteaders. The bridge provided safe access to the districts being settled on the west side of the river. It is now necessary to travel over six miles to view the Stephansson Cenotaph, located directly across the river. This cenotaph at the poet's gravesite was erected in 1936, funded in the depths of the Great Depression by admirers of his literary achievements and his philosophy in Canada, the United States and Iceland, without governmental assistance.

A walking bridge would allow visitors to Stephansson House to walk from Hola School to view the cenotaph in the cemetery. Hola School typically illustrates the one room schools that served the Canadian prairie farm families for grades one to five from soon after the turn of the century until the mid-fifties.

Yours truly, Stephan V. Benediktson

Chapter 31

The Hecla School District

By Darwin Baker and Stephan V. Benediktson

This is how a rural Alberta community, the Hecla District, established schools for their children in the early years. The eastern boundary of the Hecla District was the Medicine River some ten miles west of Innisfail, Alberta. Both of the writers' grandparents were among the first group of settlers in the district and their descendants have lived and farmed in this area ever since.[1]

Two groups of Icelanders settled northeast of Hecla in the Markerville District in the 1880s, the first in 1888 and the second in 1889. Bridges were constructed over both the Red Deer and Medicine Rivers west of Innisfail, largely as a result of the Icelandic settlers. Markerville had a store and a post office. The nearest doctor was in Innisfail, some 15 miles to the east.

In 1901, eleven men from Omaha, Nebraska filed for homesteads in what became the school districts of Hecla, Spruce View, Craig and Markerville. That area became known as "Yankee Flats". These Nebraskans decided to immigrate to Canada, it seems, on the promise of a homestead for $10. The eleven men went back to Nebraska; nine of them returned with their families in 1902 and the other two in 1903.

Early records in the Department of Lands and Forests indicate that about the same time three Icelandic families filed on homesteads in the district; two of the families arrived directly

---

[1]Stephan V. Benediktson's paternal grandparents arrived in the district directly from Iceland in 1902. Stephan, born June 22, 1933 on the Benediktson homestead one mile south of Hecla School, started school at Hecla in September, 1938 and graduated from Grade 9 at the Tindastoll School in the Markerville District, in June, 1947. While in Grade 5 at Hecla School his teacher arbitrarily transferred Stephan into Grade 6, saving him one full year.

from Iceland and the other family arrived via the United States. One Swedish family arrived from the United States in 1902 and another Swedish family in 1903. These early settlers travelled by train to Innisfail and then on to their homesteads by horse and wagon.

The homesteads were tree covered, and the settlers faced the challenge of clearing the land to farm it. The families living in the north-east part of the community sent their children to schools that had been established by the Icelanders at Tindastoll and Hola. Roads were almost non-existent, and as the schools were eight to ten miles away, the children missed a lot of school in the winter months.

In 1902 the people of Yankee Flats built a log cabin they called Bethel on the South East Quarter of Section 30, Township 36 that served as both a church and a schoolhouse. Amanda Anderson, a daughter of one of the Nebraska settlers, had attended school in Omaha and so became the first teacher. There were approximately 12 students and Amanda was paid by a collection from the families. This school was never registered as such, and when the Bethel Church was built half a mile west of the original log cabin, classes were held there until the Hecla School was built in 1904.

The location of the school was a problem, and it was not possible to please everyone. According to the Federal Act of 1896, the government reserved Sections 11 and 29 in each township to be used for educational purposes. In many cases, such as Hecla, the settlers did not live near Sections 11 or 29; 11 was in the south-east and 29 was in the extreme north. The problem was settled characteristically when Johann Bjarnason, an Icelandic settler, donated an acre of land in the North West corner of Section 10, Township 36, Range 2, West of the 5th Meridian, to build a school on. This was centrally located, and the school was named Hecla after Mount Hekla, a volcano in Iceland.

Hecla was one of 237 school districts organized in 1904 in the North West Territories and was registered as Hecla School District 1014 on April 20, 1904. The southern boundary of the district was formed by the Red Deer River, which cut off portions of Sections 3, 11, and 12 of Township 36 and Section 33 of Township 35. The boundaries excluded some of the original families to the north-west whose children continued to attend school at the Bethel Church until the Spruce View School was built in 1913.

Barney Bjarnason, a long-time School Board Chairman, recalled the first Hecla School. Barney said, "The people hired to build it did a very rough job." There was no basement, and the toilets were two small buildings in the school yard. The school was heated with a wood-burning stove with the stovepipes strung across the room to the chimney. Esther (Nelson) Baker reminisced, "I remember we used to bring our lunches in from the cloak-room to thaw out around the stove before lunch." The school water supply was courtesy of the Deckers, who lived next door.

A grant system established in 1900 provided a per diem rate of $1.20, and the teachers were paid $600 per year, from local taxation and the government grant. The first Secretary-Treasurer of the school board was John Nelson, a post he held for many years. John Nelson was a bachelor, but his contribution to the school system showed a real concern for the education of children in the area. John was succeeded by Ted Thompson. Barney Bjarnason said, "I can remember men occasionally working on the roads to pay off their taxes, but the teachers at Hecla were always paid." Education was a priority in the minds of the Hecla residents.

The first teacher at Hecla was a Mr. Richardson, an older man from Eastern Canada. Beuphard Baker said, "Maybe he'd taught somewhere before, but considering his language I doubt that he was a teacher." Beuphard was thirteen at the time and had attended school in Omaha before coming to Canada. Richardson stayed at the Nelson farm and walked the mile to school and back. Richardson's class consisted of 19 students at various stages of their education.

Hecla had a variety of teachers in the early years, albeit from a variety of places. Mr. Discher had attended a Normal School in Eastern Canada; Miss Strong was from the United States; Miss Coates was from England; Mr. Thorsteinson, an Icelander, was

The students of Heckla School with Mrs. C. Norman.
1904

from Manitoba; and Chris Christiansen was a Danish teacher
who arrived via the United States. The variety of ethnic back-
grounds of these early teachers was an education in itself; it was
not always the teacher with the highest qualifications who had
the most lasting effect on the students.

A teacher's residence was built at Hecla in 1942. Prior to
that the teachers boarded at various homes in the district: the
Nelsons, the Bakers, the Mustards and the Thompsons. The first
teachers had very little to work with but the young minds of their
students. For equipment they received a hand bell, a desk bell,
blackboard and chalk, a teacher's desk and pupil's desks, the
type where the seat of one desk was attached to the table of the
other. It was difficult to write legibly if the fellow student in the
seat in front of you was restless and moved a lot. There was no
library of any kind, and the pupils were responsible for buying
their own slates and textbooks. Esther (Nelson) Baker recalls
her yellow *Cat, Rat, Hat* book as her most prized possession
during her first years at school.

The local School Board reported to the larger board in Rocky

Mountain House, and the original school building was replaced by a new building in 1940. The Hecla District became a "spoke in the larger wheel" of the Rocky Mountain House School Division. The local delegate was Dave Pearson. All records and registers from the Hecla School were sent to the Rocky Mountain House Divisional Office where a fire destroyed all of the original records.

There were no significant changes in the education system at Hecla for the next three decades. Supplies became more readily available; the teachers were better qualified and were better paid. In 1936 the Province passed legislation enabling the Department of Education to proceed with a policy of merging school districts to form large units. The Department of Education, in proceeding with this policy, arranged to explain the intentions of the department and to discuss probable boundaries. Divisions were established by Ministerial Orders and the boundaries were determined on the basis of topography, transportation facilities, population, marketing centers and community interests.

It was decided to build a new school, and the contractor was John Hillman, a local Icelandic carpenter. The new school boasted many features not found in the old school: a full basement, chemical bathrooms, insulation, a coal furnace, a boys' cloakroom in the basement and one for the girls on the ground floor. The new school was furnished with tables and chairs instead of desks. There was no plumbing, and electricity was not available until 1950. The community was proud of their new building and felt that it would help attract teachers.

Hecla did not experience significant difficulties attracting teachers during the war years from 1939 to 1945. One year in the late 1940s the administration hired a Supervisor, Darlene Lightbowan, and used correspondence lessons. Another year in the late 1940s the school opening was delayed. A teacher from Saskatchewan, Doris Dell, a relative of the Walkers, was hired. Eleanor Pedersen was the last teacher of the Hecla School in the year 1956. For the following two years students were bussed from Dickson to Innisfail, a long tiring day for the children. The Hecla School was then used for community gatherings and church services.

Family

In 1953, several school districts, including Hecla, were transferred from the Rocky Mountain House School Division to the Red Deer School Division, and a centralized school was built at Spruce View. In 1959 the centralized school at Spruce View opened with Bill Mewha, the principal from Markerville, appointed Principal and Mr. Sloan, the principal from Dickson, appointed Vice-Principal. The Spruce View School proved too small to accommodate all the students from the area, so Grades One and Two were continued in Dickson, and Hecla was reopened to accommodate Grade Three with Miss Fitch as the teacher. A new wing was added to the school at Spruce View. The students were first bussed to Spruce View, and then Grades One and Two were sent on to Dickson and Grade Three was sent on to Hecla School.

The people in the area were indebted to the far-sighted Danish community of Dickson for establishing the first rural high school in Alberta. On August 13, 1930, the Dickson High School Association was formed with tuition fees of $40 per annum. Miss Gundersen, the daughter of the first Lutheran minister at Dickson, gave up an opportunity to teach at Alberta College to teach at the new Dickson High School. Her salary was $1,000 per year, but in actual practice she received only what was left after all of the expenses were paid. So great was her dedication to the community that she offered to work without pay. The high school was held in the basement of the first Lutheran Church at Dickson and received high school students from outside the public school district on the same terms as the local students. In the first year, 1930, Grades Ten and Eleven were offered and Grade Twelve was added the following year.

A major school problem in rural Canada was accommodation for the students, particularly girls, who lived outside the public school district. In their traditional community-minded spirit in 1933 the Danish people donated land, and a volunteer labour force began construction of a dormitory for girls. The matrons who served in the dormitory and the treatment received by the students was exemplary: "a home away from home". By 1937, the Dickson High School moved from the church basement to the dormitory with a staff of three.

The Rocky Mountain House School Division took over the operation of the Dickson High School by Ministerial Order in 1937, while the High School Association continued to operate the dormitory until 1954. In 1938, the Rocky Mountain House School Division built a new school at Dickson for Grades One to Twelve, and the High School at Dickson moved into its third home. In December 1954 the Dickson High School was transferred to the Red Deer School Division. The administration was unable to hire a Grade Twelve teacher for the 1955-56 year, so only Grades Ten and Eleven were offered. In 1959 the Dickson High School was transferred to the new Spruce View School.

Among the first Hecla School pupils who attended Dickson High School were Robert N. Thompson and Violet Larsen in 1931. After a distinguished career in Ethiopia, Robert Thompson returned to Canada where he became the leader of the federal Social Credit Party and Violet Larsen became Dr. Violet Lund, a well-known and highly regarded Saskatchewan doctor.

Chapter 32

Retirement and Polo

It was in the spring of 2000 that my sister Iris came for the weekend. We were selling the oil company and had decided to take
up residency in a warmer climate; we had not decided exactly
where, other than it would be in a Latin country. I like a lot of
things about Latin America: the good manners, eating late, the
music, the service, playing polo, etc. Also, my wife, Adriana, is
a Latina, born and raised in Colombia from a Dutch father and
a Colombian mother. I must confess there is a certain amount
of flexibility in Latin America that appeals to me also.

Iris asked me what I was going to do with my string of polo
ponies. I was down to five very special ponies; four were born
and bred at Benson Ranch from polo-playing mothers that I had
brought from Argentina when I returned to Canada in 1987.
Pumita, Estriellita, Palomita and Ventanita were daughters of
Puma, Estriella, Paloma and Ventana. The fifth, which I called
T-bone, because of an early incident, was a local product of
thoroughbred breeding that had the same calm mind-set of the
others, was the same size and generally the same color. They
were amazing.

I told Iris I could not bring myself to sell them. I told her
about Carlos and Eduardo, Mexican brothers from Queretaro,
Mexico, who had traveled to Grande Prairie, Alberta to visit
Cled and Loretta Lewis the past summer and had stopped at
Benson Ranch for a few days *en route*. They were just starting in polo and typically had caught the polo bug but did not
have playing polo horses. I had played at their club, Balvanera,
in Queretaro. In fact the owner, Shepo de Alba, had flown to
Calgary in his plane, with his wife, his mother, his polo pro, An-

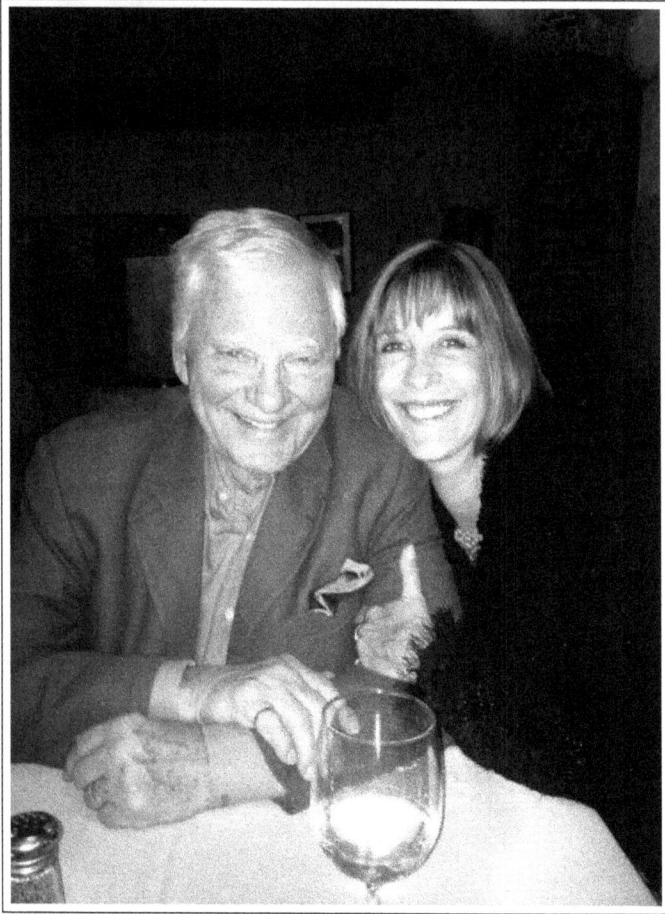

Stephan and Adriana

tonio (Chumuko) Herrera and another couple the previous year to visit and play polo with his friend from Grande Praire, Cled Lewis.

We have a polo field at Benson Ranch near Cochrane, Alberta, and as a result Cled called me to explain and suggest that rather than Shepo and his group traveling from Calgary to Grande Prairie, that the Grande Prairie team travel to Benson

Family

Ranch and play Shepo's team there, which they did. On a beautiful Alberta day in August, blue skies and sunshine, Shepo, An-
tonio, Jose Sauza and I successfully overcame the Grande Prairie
challenge made up of Cled, Murray Sutherland, Ross Adams and
Bill Stinchcome.

Cledwyn Lewis is a charming Welshman, an easy talker with
an easy manner. Cled is a medical doctor who after a career
in the British military moved to Grande Prairie, Alberta. Cled
missed his polo playing days, so he set about motivating and
training a group of Grande Prairie horse people, mostly cowboys,
including his wife Loretta, to play polo. Cled with a number of
his protégés would go on tour to play polo, occasionally in the
summer and usually once in the winter to such places as Buenos
Aires, Argentina or British Guiana, West Africa or Queretaro,
Mexico. In fact Adriana and I joined them on their second trip
to Queretaro, during which one boisterous day off from polo we
wed Cled and Loretta in Macarena's restaurant in San Miguel
de Allende. Their marital status had always been of concern to
Adriana, a good Catholic girl, so Macarena told her that the
dentist down the street, Jose, was a Justice of Peace and could
come after work and officiate. Murray Sutherland supported the
groom and all had a good time.

I told Iris that I had entered into an arrangement with Carlos,
one of the young Mexican polo players from Queretaro, whereby
I would deliver my ponies and horse trailer to El Paso, Texas
and sell him my horse trailer. Carlos would pick up the horses
and trailer there and take them to the Balvanera Club, and use
them as his own. I would come and play them from time to
time. As it turned out, we retired in 2002 to San Miguel de
Allende, 45 minutes from the Balvenera Club, so until I had a
big wreck in 2005 I played them a lot. I told Iris I was looking
for someone to drive my truck and trailer to El Paso and then
drive the truck back. I had wanted to do the trip with Adriana
and to spend a few days in Santa Fe, New Mexico on the return
trip, but Adriana was less than enthusiastic about the idea. I
told Iris I was talking to some rancher friends around Cochrane
about doing the run for me, and my 77 year old sister Iris said

look no farther: "I am going to do that trip." Accordingly, one chilly fall morning I loaded my fabulous five, drove to the door, Iris got in and drove off. She picked up her friend Betty en route at Ft. MacLeod and five days later called me from El Paso to tell me that she had found the stable to leave the horses at and asked me how to disconnect the trailer.

I asked Adriana, "What do you think of retiring to Buenos Aires?" I love the city, having lived there for several years in the 80s. When I said, "If it doesn't work for you we won't stay," she agreed. In due course, we arrived in Buenos Aires where the country was in one of its major financial crisis, a reoccurring condition. The peso had been pegged to the dollar, and Argentine products were so expensive that they could not export anything. As a result there was over 20% unemployment and many hungry people demonstrating in the streets, pounding pots and pans; robberies were not uncommon. After three days Adriana announced, "This does not work for me." I kept her there for four months, but she never changed her mind, so we returned to our apartment in Atlanta.

On a subsequent trip to Queretaro to play polo in October 2001, we revisited San Miguel de Allende where we chanced on a house we liked, bought it, and San Miguel has been our base ever since. It was everything we had hoped for, plus I could drive to Queretaro, in more or less 45 minutes, and play polo three or four times a week at Balvanera.

In the winter of 2005 Iris came to visit. At a polo match on a beautiful sunny Sunday with Iris and some friends watching, we played a very competitive tournament. I played Pumita in the fifth chucker, she was a very good player and probably the fastest polo horse in Mexico. I outdid myself in a play from one end of the field to the other, "coast to coast" as we say. Nobody could catch us as I covered the field in five hits and drove the ball through the goal posts, with seven players in hot pursuit. I turned Pumita slightly out of the line, and for some reason that I have never understood we went down at full speed, my life passing before my eyes. I lay for a moment, taking inventory, then got up. To my great surprise and pleasure I was unhurt

Benediktson At Seniors Polo Tournament.
El Dorado Polo Club, Palm Desert, March 2008

but could not understand why Pumita made no effort to get up until I saw her front leg. It was dangling; the bone was broken completely in two. Unfortunately the field was somewhat uneven, which combined with our turn lead to this disaster.

I walked around taking stock, considering my 72 years at the time, my years of playing this fascinating game, what it would be like to spend my last few years in a wheel chair dependent on someone to take care of me, and I decided to quit polo. I have played polo a few times since in the Seniors Tournament at Palm Desert in 2005 and 2008. All of the emotions, good feelings, adrenalin rushes and thrills were still there. In fact I had the dubious distinction of being awarded the prize for being the oldest player in the tournament each time. The last time, in 2008, we lost four goals to five to a team of 50 year olds.

One of the retirement projects that I have enjoyed being associated with has been the establishment of two fellowships at the Banff Centre. The Banff Centre, founded in the year of my birth, 1933, was highly regarded by my mother Rosa. The school exists to inspire leaders and artists to make their unique contributions to society. As a creative and educational institution, it has innovative programs that develop artists and leaders, is a catalyst for creativity in a unique environment in the Canadian Rockies with special learning opportunities, outreach activities and performances for the public.

Some years ago Adriana and I established a fellowship at the Banff Centre for one Icelandic artist each year, to honor the ethnic background that I am so proud off, and some years later we established a fellowship there for one Mexican artist per year, in appreciation of our pleasant retirement years in the artist colony San Miguel de Allende, Mexico.

Part 4

Contrarian Views

Chapter 33

Canada's Colonial Status

Since I've been old enough to think for myself I've asked myself, "Why is Canada a colony?" I think, "Singapore left the Commonwealth of Nations fifty years ago and has functioned successfully ever since. If Iceland can make it on their own with 300,000 people, why can't Canada?"

This used to be very, very important to me when I was young. When we got together with friends and family I would start on this. At first most people would say, "We're not a colony," and I would reply, "Read your passport." The passport reads, "– in the name of Her Majesty the Queen, all those whom it may concern to allow the bearer to pass freely –." Usually the person involved would read their passport and report back to me with chagrin, "We are still a colony."

I've spent a little time in some sovereign nations that love their royalty; the Dutch love their Queen, which is understandable since their Queen is Dutch. Our Queen is not even Canadian.

In conversation on the subject, friends and family's eyes would glaze over – "Not that again." I reluctantly concluded that Canadians, with the possible exception of some French Canadians, don't really care.

I have the greatest admiration for the British; it's not that. My first wife was born in London, so I have had some connection with this whole thing; they are an amazing people. A few thousand Brits with fur hats and bagpipes controlled several million people in India for years.

In later years I have decided this isn't a cause worth getting really serious about. A friend of mine gave me something I can live with when he said, "Steve, just think of it as a Rent a Queen program." Why not?

Chapter 34

Government Spending

Government spending is far too high and in my opinion frequently borders on the ridiculous. Government spending is too often directed to "buying votes" rather than investing in the practical and necessary. This is a direct result of our democratic system, the best system we have been able to come up with to date but far from perfect. I seriously dislike deficit budgeting, seemingly a routine in our system.

Alberta's government is a prime example; they have funded a magnesium plant where there is no magnesium, destroyed hospitals in order to justify new hospitals. Each year they remove miles of perfectly good road and street surfaces and resurface them, build town halls that are used infrequently, and build fences between two roads. They have now built a new hospital in Grande Prairie, Alberta, at a cost of some $475 million, that one medical practitioner there has assured me they did not need. The Canadian Museum for Human Rights recently completed in Winnipeg was originally budgeted for $212 million and finally cost $357 million, an awesome project, but we cannot help but wonder if the Canadian taxpayer could really afford it and if that money would not have been better directed towards paying down debt. The list goes on. These projects are politically motivated not economically motivated.

The worst example of incompetence in Alberta has been the Alberta Heritage Fund. Set up by the newly elected party in Alberta in 1971 to ensure the financial future of Albertans, the fund has a value of some $17.5 billion as compared to the Norwegian Sovereign Fund, set up around the same time, set up around the same time, which has some $880 billion. Norway has a population similar to Alberta. The difference is that Norway prohibited access to their fund by politicians, whereas in Alberta the same political party used the Alberta fund as a piggy bank for their ridiculous spending.

In my opinion, civil servant salaries are too high and the civil service is over staffed. I recall in Argentina when President Mennem asked Pepe Estensoro to become the President of the national oil company, YPF, they had 35,000 employees. A few years later when they sold the company they had 8,000 employees. It's called "biting the bullet", and it needs top level support. We seem to forget the truism that the consumer pays; all costs are passed on to the consumer.

The United States should make it illegal to spend more than a few million dollars per party on any given election campaign and make it illegal to campaign for politics until a few months prior to an election.

The Federal Government in the United States has a major problem with their State Governments in regard to control, most particularly in regard to health care and education. There is an urgent need to standardize health care and education in the United States, but the State Governments successfully block standardization in order to maintain their control. As a result, health care is over priced in the United States and the standard of education had fallen to the level of third world countries.

It would seem that in most democratic countries, the elected leaders can arrange to pass a law standardizing the level of education across their country, as is the case in Canada. This does not seem possible in the United States.[1] Similarly, it would seem that the elected leader of a democracy should be able to arrange for a law standardizing health care for a medical plan across their country, as Canada has. Unfortunately, President Obama could not get that done in the United States.

---

[1]See Peter Elkind, "Business Gets Schooled," *Fortune Magazine* (January 1, 2016).

Chapter 35

Democracy

In our democratic system political leaders promise more and more spending of the taxpayers' money on unnecessary social programs or accepting ever more refugees, etc, simply to buy votes. The refugee problem needs to be solved in the refugee's country of origin as in most cases the refugees do not want to leave their home countries. The cost of politicking, particularly in the United States is ludicrous, absolutely ridiculous. These funds would be better directed to paying down government debts.

In 1887 Alexander Tyler, a Scottish history professor at the University of Edinburgh, had this to say about the fall of the Athenian Republic some 2,000 years prior: "A democracy is always temporary in nature; it simply cannot exist as a permanent form of government. A democracy will continue to exist up until the time the voters discover that they can vote for themselves generous gifts from the public treasury. From that moment on, the majority always vote for the candidate who promises the most benefits from the public treasury, with the result that every democracy will finally collapse over loose fiscal policy, always followed by a dictatorship."

We should consider an alternate form of government. I would suggest that a form of government based on the corporate model could be much better. I believe the Chinese system operates on somewhat of the corporate model. The people in charge must "earn their spurs" so as to speak. Proven management are progressively promoted to higher levels of authority; expenditures are based on the economic merits of each project. In our democratic system people are elected from the "great unwashed" – pig farmers, charismatic students, lawyers, etc – who are no more qualified to govern than you or I. The taxpaying public deserves better.

Chapter 36

Resource Planning

There is a serious lack of planning in our democratic form of government. Elected delegates have a four or five year term, and as result long term planning is not a priority, getting re-elected is. There is a pressing need for long term planning, particularly for food, water and energy. I wrote a paper on Population Pressures in 1962 when the world population was 3 billion people. Today, in 2016, we have 7 billion people, and experts project that in 2050 we will have 9 billion people; think about it.

I grew up on a farm in Central Alberta. In 1950 the principal grain crops were wheat, barley and oats, and the prices were more or less $2.50, $1.50 and $1.00 per bushel, respectively. These prices stayed about the same for almost 60 years until now, driven by supply and demand, they have essentially tripled. With the world's ever increasing population driving demand, there needs to be a significant effort put into long range planning for global food supplies.

Pope Frances recently commented that the world must stop wasting so much food. He pointed out that the United States, with four percent of the world's population, consumes twenty five percent of the world's food production and wastes twenty percent of what it consumes. Coincidentally, the United States, with four percent of the world's population, consumes twenty percent of the world's oil and gas production.

Water supply has already surfaced as a serious problem in California, Arizona, Texas and Northern Mexico. Beef production has been drastically reduced in these areas. In Western Canada cow-calf operators traditionally wean and sell their calves in the fall. In the past they could expect a 500 pound calf to sell for $1.00 per pound. In the fall of 2014 producers were getting as high as $2.50 per pound for their calves.

Global warming is happening, glaciers are melting and our sources of fresh water are draining into the oceans. There has been a focused effort to play down global warming, particularly by the petroleum industry which does not wish to accept the consequences of green-house gas emissions.

I first visited Lake Louise in Alberta some 70 years ago. When I looked across the lake I saw a wall of ice, a glacier, dripping water into the lake.Today when you walk up to the lake you can see a few blocks of glacial ice on the mountain across the lake.

In 1965 I drove across the Texas Panhandle en route to my next posting in Houston. The Panhandle was dotted with windmills pumping water for the cattle from more or less 200 feet. Today there are no wind mills in the Panhandle. The ranchers are pumping water with electric submersible pumps from several hundred feet down, where they can.

The agriculture industry has historically enjoyed preferential water rights, and in many cases they use the water very inefficiently, unchallenged. Spray irrigation systems are a flagrant waste of water. The flow of water in the major rivers of the world such as the Mississippi and the Ganges has diminished significantly with time.

Much can and needs to be done to conserve water. People need to change their lifestyles to conserve energy and to protect the environment. The twentieth century was possibly the century with the most remarkable advances that Planet Earth will ever experience, and we were there. We went from cars to computers with everything in between – flight, medical advances, walks on the moon, etc.

I would suggest that the twenty-first century is going to end much differently. Population pressures will result in global shortages of resources, some of which are already happening. Consider people's reactions to global shortages of food, water and energy; most people will go to any extreme for food and water for their children.

Chapter 37

Oil and Gas Policy

In my opinion Canada does not need any more pipelines to export oil and gas. We are dealing with a wasting asset here: once you use it, it is gone and cannot be replenished. The price is only going to go up (notwithstanding short-term aberrations such as the break through in developing shale oil, horizontal drilling, and hydraulic fracturing), so what is the rush to sell of an asset that can only grow in value over time? There is a great deal of pressure to increase exports, in large part because of the demand for oil and gas in the United States.

The press and the American political system do a remarkable job of presenting the American oil and gas supply-demand situation in a positive light, but the facts are that today the United States uses upwards of 20 million barrels of oil per day and, including the past few years development of shale oil and production increases through horizontal drilling and fracking, the United States produces in the order of 10 million barrels of oil per day, up from 5 million barrels per day. The United States was self-sufficient in oil until 1955 when demand exceeded 10 million barrels per day.

For those who have taken comfort from the various sources who in the past few years allude to the advances in developing oil and gas from shale formations, I would suggest they read *Cold Hungry and in the Dark* by Bill Powers. In his well-researched and documented book, Powers explodes the myth that shale gas could supply Americans with gas for the next 100 years. At today's rate of consumption Powers calculates that shale gas reserves could provide some six years supply of gas for Americans compared to the 100 years supply put forward by various industry experts.

When I started working in the oil industry in Alberta in the 1950s, the practice was to reserve a twenty year supply of conventional reserves for domestic consumption. The National Energy Board of the day carefully considered all applications to export oil and gas. This policy changed drastically with the change of government in Alberta in 1971. The policy became, "Let's go to the bank today," by producing and selling as much oil and gas as possible. As a result, today Alberta has less than a six-year supply of conventional oil reserves and some eight years' supply of natural gas reserves based on the current rate of consumption in Canada. The needs of future generations of Canadians are seldom mentioned.

So-called alternate energies will provide minor amounts of global energy needs. Coal is the most significant alternate energy source but is also non-renewable and produces significant amounts of CO_2 emissions when it is burned. Nuclear energy is similarly bracketed, as there is a finite amount of fissionable material on the planet. Like oil and gas there is a finite amount of all of the natural resources on planet earth, and as these resources are consumed they are not replenished.

Chapter 38

Palestinian Situation

Until I went to work in Saudi Arabia for Aramco I was generally aware of the Palestinian situation without having thought seriously about it. When I was placed in charge of one of Aramco's producing divisions I had a number of Palestinians working under me and came to realize these people do not have a country. After the Second World War the whole world was understandably in a state of abject remorse over the Holocaust, an unbelievable atrocity, and the international community under the League of Nations in 1947 put the Palestinians out of what had been their country for over 2,000 years and gave it to the Jewish people.

In 1975 we visited Jordon and one morning there we hired a taxi to take us to Petra, which was a famous isolated hub on the caravan routes from East to West dating back to biblical times. To that time the only way to enter Petra was to travel on foot or on a horse several miles down a canyon. We elected to ride horses in and stayed in the only accommodation there, cave like rooms carved into the side of the cliffs. We listened to hyena's howling during the night. Our dinner was cooked over a camp fire and the taxi driver slept in his taxi at the entrance waiting for our return the next day. On the return trip to Amman, we took the opportunity to swim in the Dead Sea, 1,400 feet below sea level, a unique experience because the water is so heavily laden with salt that you float.

We visited the West Bank from Jordan, and I saw firsthand how the displaced Palestinians are forced to live, in squalid card board shacks with no services or proper sanitation. Several generations of Palestinians, these angry young men you can see on the news throwing rocks, have been born and raised in these appalling conditions. As I watched the planes fly into the twin towers in New York on television in 1997 it seemed to me to be a statement to the world, "Do something!"

Do not misunderstand, that particular atrocity was unjustified, but it was a response to an unbelievable injustice that has existed now for upwards of 70 years, and the situation remains unresolved as a direct result of the American support of Israel. As Thomas L. Friedman says in his book, *From Beirut to Jerusalem*, "America gives $3 billion a year to Israel because of the electoral clout with Congress." This injustice to the Palestinians and the over whelming American and now Canadian support for Israel has led to the point where the Moslem world continues to demand justice more and more aggressively.

President Obama declared early in his term that "the borders of Israel and Palestine should be based on the 1967 lines with mutually agreed swaps, so that secure and recognized borders are established for both states." This simple and obvious action would finally establish a Palestinian country. The Arab world is waiting for a solution to this complex problem.

Without a doubt the world would have been a safer place with less conflict and killing had a more thoughtful League of Nations in 1947 not carved out a province somewhere else to call Israel, rather than displacing the Palestinians and creating a Jewish state surrounded by Moslem countries. Friedman states, "Had the early Zionists taken up the British offer to establish their state in Uganda instead of in the holy land, news from Israel might have been a little less interesting."

Chapter 39

Indigenous Policy

Canada's Native peoples are by and large a tragedy; it could and should be so different. The Government of Canada's policies for native people are completely out of touch with what needs to be done. In my opinion, the Native peoples need to be integrated into life in Canada. These people will never change until they have to support themselves, like the rest of society. If they have to, they can and they will. The policy of "throwing money at it" does not work. Canada is dotted with abandoned projects, expensive projects, for the Natives that probably seemed like a good thing to do at the time but did not work.

Just one example of these misguided bureaucratic spending projects is the Nakoda Lodge west of Cochrane, Alberta. Well-designed and located, built with public funds and gifted to the local tribe, the Nakoda Lodge was operated by the Natives for several years and is now shut down because they were unable to operate the lodge profitably. Similar projects with similar results can be found across Canada.

The existing Native Band establishments in Native communities are rife with favouritism and financial abuse; the system is not working. According to *MacLean's* magazine, January 12, 2015, some 170 Chiefs are pulling down over six figures, a direct cost to Canadian tax payers. Meanwhile 39% of the on-reserve students in Alberta have dropped out of school. Only 48.5% of Alberta's Aboriginal population have high school diplomas, compared to 80% percent of the Non-Aboriginal population.

Certainly the Canadian Government must continue to recognize and fulfill all constitutional and treaty obligations. I worked in Ottawa for two years in the Department of Indian and North-

160

ern Affairs. With all due respect, Canada's Native population needs to "get a job," to go to work like the rest of us. There is a school of thought that believes we are here on earth to work, to do something with our lives. Certainly no group is here to exist at the expense of society as a whole.

Chapter 40

The Death Penalty

A Gallup survey conducted in October, 2015, confirmed that 60 percent of Americans support capital punishment. I also believe in capital punishment, that the death penalty should be the rule worldwide. In addition to what I feel is the compelling logic of this position, I have two reasons of precedent for saying this.

Firstly, when the Western States were settled, a man's horse was vital for survival as there were no alternate methods of transportation. A man's horse was so important for survival that they hanged horse thieves, and that punishment significantly helped to control the crime of stealing horses.

Secondly, I lived for quite a number of years in Moslem countries and found them to be very law-abiding, the atrocious activities of ISIS, an extremist minority, in recent years the exception. This is because of the principle of "an eye for an eye." From what I know about the Moslem religion, both the law and the religion are contained in the *Koran*. For example, the *Koran* says that you shall not kill or you will be killed. Traditionally, if someone killed someone and if it was witnessed and obvious, that person was beheaded before the sun went down the same day; there is nothing to talk about. You do not need a lawyer or the kind of defence and legal system that freed O. J. Simpson.

Consider whether Russell Williams of the Canadian military, who confessed to two horrible murders, two home invasion sexual assaults and dozens of break ins, should have been executed rather than sent to prison with the chance of parole after twenty-five years.

Another example I have found hard to accept was that in late 2014, the President of Colombia, very strangely, pardoned a guerrilla chief, Vasquez, one of Carlos Escobar's leaders. Vasquez killed hundreds of people, was caught and sentenced to thirty years in prison. Vasquez was released and in fact is now free to arrange the execution of those who collaborated on his conviction. This has been a major disincentive for Colombian policemen since the International Community successfully lobbied the Colombian Government to abolish the death penalty for humanitarian reasons some thirty years ago.

Think about it.

Chapter 41

Gun Control in the United States

It should be made illegal to own a gun or rifle in the United States, as in many other countries, except of course with permits for hunters and for collectors. Americans adamantly support their frontier position that all people should have the right to carry a fire arm to defend themselves, by shooting any attackers, I suppose. As a result hardly a week goes by without some malcontent in the United States opening fire on some group, be they in restaurants, military, students or church groups, and killing many and maiming more. Taking away the constitutional right to own a firearm would seem to be a small price to pay for reducing the carnage.

In 2015 one malcontent opened fire on a church group killing nine and maiming many more. In the headlines reporting the incident the next day one newspaper made a serious case for allowing preachers to have pistols in their pulpits to deal with such circumstances. There was no mention of gun control. Can you imagine shoot outs in the House of God?

Chapter 42

NAFTA

The idea of a North American Free Trade Agreement was first put forward in the late 1980s with great enthusiasm. I gave the concept some very serious thought and came to the conclusion that it would be sort of win-lose for the USA and win-win for Mexico and lose-lose for Canada, largely for two very fundamental reasons, one related to manufacturing and the other related to agriculture.

In the manufacturing industry, no company would build and operate a plant in Canada if they could serve the same market from a plant in Mexico, because of the Canadian climate and the high costs of Canadian labour. The cost to build and operate a plant in Canada is multiples higher than an equivalent plant in Mexico. Since NAFTA, the Canadian government, in their wisdom and with no regard for taxpayers' money, have induced various manufacturers to build plants in Canada by paying the major cost of their plants. They are now paying hundreds of millions of taxpayers' dollars to keep the plants operating in Canada rather than manufacturing in Mexico, in large part a result of the NAFTA agreement.

In agriculture, Canada does an amazing job of competing considering the Canadian climate. Canadian grain growers must deal with the short growing-season between frosts, hail storms and occasional droughts. The southern states and Mexico have no major frost problems. In some places in the world, such as the Pampa in Argentina, they have no drought, frost, or hail problems and take two crops off per year. Canadian beef producers must put up feed and physically feed their cattle for six months of the year, whereas in the southern states and Mexico cattle range out all year long. The beef producers there do not have the expense of putting up hay or feeding their cattle over the winter months.

The NAFTA agreement required that all producers and growers in each country relinquish all subsidies and benefits. The Canadian producers did so, but the American agriculture producers, the heaviest subsidized industry on the planet, have not. No one, not politicians or union leaders or NAFTA, seem to have the ability to reduce the subsidies to American agriculture producers.

I have not changed my position on NAFTA.

Chapter 43

Mexico Environmentally

Mexico is the most environmentally polluted country on Planet Earth. People still throw their garbage in plastic bags out along the roads and throw their trash on the ground wherever they are standing or driving. The problem is compounded by the apparent lack of concern for the problem by succeeding generations of administrations, municipal, provincial and federal, and the lack of infrastructure necessary to deal with garbage collection and disposal. There are very few garbage containers, few garbage collection services or well organized and administrated garbage dumps. Wherever you go in Mexico you will find garbage strewn as far as the eye can see.

I have lived and worked in nine different countries, North and South America, the Middle East and the Far East included, and have travelled extensively, and Mexico is the most casually polluting country in the world. The problem is a matter of educating the public and providing the infrastructure to collect and dispose of garbage. I recall the "Don't Be a Litter Bug," campaign in Canada presented to children in the schools in the 1940s after the Second World War. The children served to police their parents whenever they were tempted to throw their cigarette packages or whatever out of the car windows.

I have visited mining operations in remote locations in Mexico where I thought the environment was pristine, only to look down and see bottles and plastic wrappings strewn all over the ground. In Durango Province there are miles of barbed wire fences on the ranches and the wind blows constantly. The fences are solid sheets of plastics, blown by the wind and caught on the wires.

Restless as a Viking

There are a lot of things I like about Mexico; I have lived in Mexico some fourteen years. I mention the problem because I care and I cannot understand the indifference to such a serious problem in a country where jobs are important and salaries are low. A major labour force could be employed at a modest cost to clean up the Mexican environment and to install the requisite infra-structure. With present day media coverage, a program to educate the public with respect to the basics of environmental protection would be very easy to create and to present to the public. This should be a national priority.

Chapter 44

Corporate America

Corporate America's excesses, particularly with regard to executive compensation, are a disgrace and particularly insulting to working classes the world over. No individual anywhere on this planet is worth the outrageously high salaries Corporate America pays themselves. I have been an officer of an American Fortune 500 company. No one individual should receive the outrageously high salary and bonuses that these people are awarding themselves; none of these people are worth such high costs. The fact is that the consumer pays all corporate costs, not the corporation; all costs are passed on to the consumer, including such excesses as executive compensation. It would not be unreasonable for the government of United States to pass a law limiting executive compensation to protect the consuming public. A limit of say possibly ten million dollars per year, salary and bonus could be considered; no one deserves the 50 to 70 million dollar awards that are being paid these days from any organization.

I spent upwards of 20 years working for Exxon companies. A contemporary of mine went on to become the CEO of Exxon and severed admirably as such for many years. When he retired some 15 years ago he received a well-publicised severance package of over $400 million; such is Corporate America. I am sure he could have lived out his retirement years very nicely at that stage with $10 million and Exxon could have reduced the cost of gasoline at the pumps by some fraction of a cent for the next number of years with the $390 million saved.

Index

About the Author

Stephan V. Benediktson is an engineering graduate of the University of Alberta. Stephan spent upwards of 20 years in resident assignments with affiliates of Exxon, in Canada, the USA, Australia, Indonesia and Saudi Arabia, as well as two years with Northern Development Canada, regulating exploration drilling in the Beaufort Sea. Stephan was a Vice President of Amerada Hess Corp and managed their operations in the UAE, served as the Director General of Bridas SAPIC in Argentina, was the Founder and CEO of Benson Petroleum Ltd. and the Co-Founder and CEO of PetroSantander Inc. Stephan now resides with his wife, Adriana, in San Miguel de Allende, Mexico.